I Never Expected This Good Life

I Never Expected This Good Life

poems and stories

Jennifer Futernick

2011 · Capra Press, San Francisco

Copyright © 2011 by Jennifer Futernick
All rights reserved
Printed in the United States of America

ISBN: 978-1-59266-101-5

Library of Congress Control Number: 2011940101

Published by Capra Press
San Francisco, California
http://caprapress.net

Book design: Eric Larson, Studio E Books, Santa Barbara

Cover artwork: *Self-Portrait as Flame (Rose Skirt)* by Julie Heffernan
photographed by Margaret Fox

for Bob

You don't put your life into your books.
You find it there.

The Uncommon Reader

Contents

Speak of Love 3

Family

Gone 7
As We Scatter, We Return 9
Graveside 12
The Arc of a Single Shooting Star 14
The Knitter 18
The Floor Froze 21
Sleeping with My Mother 22
As If These Toes 23
My Mother's Mattress 25
Summer Heat 26
The Heartwork of O. Henry 27
Former Sister-in-Law 29
Double Mocha 30
Lanolin, or What Sisters Do 31
The Feeling of Hands 36
The Rich Scent of Pine-Sol 38
This Name 40
Heart's Geography 42

Marriage

Love Tourette's 49
Go with Bob 52
A Provident Liquor Store 59
End of an Argument 63
Flannel 64
Harmony Broke Out 65
Bed School 67
When One Weeps, the Other Tastes Salt 69
If You'd Be My Old Man, I'd Be Your Sea 71
Selecting Wallpaper 72

Children

Disappearing the Night Frost 77

Air Baseball 78

Carful of Boy, 1994 79

My Son's Heartbeat 82

My Daughter and Water 84

Night Child 86

Lace 87

Retrieving Children's Blocks at 6 A.M. 88

Bird and Nest 89

Body

Private Parts 93

Spine 94

Decrements of Pain 96

Get Well Soon 98

Surgery/Insomnia 100

The Day of Your Mastectomy 101

Perfect Boy 102

Blood in the Water 103

Dress Rehearsal 104

Faith

The Gold Filling 107

Imaginary Seder 109

Photosynthesis 112

What Was, Was, and Is No More 114

Saying Farewell to Joshua 118

Yes 121

Outside

Old-Fashioned Library 125
Making 126
Earthquake 128
Winona Ryder's Shopping Cart 135
Heavenly Taxonomy 136
Heart Sandwich 137
Lunch Alone on the Deck 139
Rewriting Hawaii 140
New Year Poems, Twenty-two Years Apart 143

Work

Working Mom 149
Analysis 151
Inventory 152
Librarian! 156
More Literate Than Numerate 159
Value-Added 163
Immersed in the Printed Word 165

Epilogue

Speak of Love, Reprise 169
Astonishment's Cup 170

Acknowledgments 173
Notes 175

I Never Expected This Good Life

Speak of Love

THE NINETEENTH-CENTURY Scottish historian, Thomas Carlyle, wrote in an essay on biography: "A loving heart is the beginning of all knowledge." A loving heart is something I was fortunate to be born with, and love is the ocean I try to swim in every day. But love can be confounding and elusive.

In 1967, when I was seventeen and nearing the end of my freshman year in college, I was taking a shower at the dorm and started to cry uncontrollably. I had this powerful sense, as if a lightning bolt had just hit, that I was not going to have a good life. The sorrows of my early years had gathered, insistently, and I was finding it difficult to breathe. I sensed that I would never experience adult love, and the years before me would be filled with loneliness. I would never get married, have children, pursue a career, live in one place, or partake in life's richness. This realization did not feel melodramatic or like the usual teen angst; it just felt overwhelmingly sad.

I have finally located, as an adult, the stability and steady love I craved when I was younger. Now, sometimes in the middle of the night I cannot sleep because I am so surprised about the way my life turned out.

When I was thirty-nine, I started writing. First a Valentine's Day poem for my husband Bob, and then poems and stories about my children, parents, siblings, and other people I love. A few years later I began writing a series of Op-Ed pieces for *The San Francisco Examiner* and realized that my life was the subject I liked to write about. These published pieces, and more recent stories, too, would have a melancholy or turbulent beginning but end on a note of harmony and the sound of hopefulness. The same was true of my poems.

As I saw many of these pages shape into something like a memoir, I had a revelation. In writing about my life, I could finally believe in the bounty that *is* my life. As I have nestled into a greater sense of security about this good life—one that I have also worked hard to nourish and sustain—I know that gratitude is the part of my heart I most wish to exercise. I wish to speak of love.

Family

As We Scatter, We Return

Gone

I dreamed he came back
dressed as Li'l Abner,
Mother was Daisy Mae.
That dream was so ridiculous
but no harder to believe
than the way he left—
gone to work with a few morning kisses
and then gone,
the foreman at the factory catching his fall
as his heart stopped.
I was in fourth grade, learning geography.

A message came over the classroom loudspeaker—
Jennifer Krames: Make sure to go straight home from school.
I wanted to go to my girlfriend Lois's house, though,
and went home with her instead. Her mother,
startled to see me because she knew,
asked if I would like to take a shower.
What a ridiculous question I thought.
She drove me home, trying to sound relaxed.

When I got home, Mother wasn't there
and I knew something was wrong
when her two friends waiting for me
looked at me with kindness, not reproof.
Your father is sick, they said,
which wasn't true because
he was already dead.

When Mother arrived, she was barely able to stand.
Her legs were rubbery and her eyes kept closing.
My young mother, always rooted in the ground
seemed to be floating, febrile.

Then I knew what had happened.

The funeral was a frozen frame
from a strangely pleasant dream.
I remember wearing new white socks
and getting kisses
and seeing so many people I liked
in one overflowing room.

From my front-row seat
I had a perfect view of his face.
He looked peaceful, which wasn't unusual
and sleeping, which seemed normal,
and handsome, which he was.
It's just that he wasn't really there.

As We Scatter, We Return

In the five-by-seven black-and-white photograph the image is blurred,
three people moving in real time.

Early September 1958, my brother Larry is boarding the train
that will take him to college, first year at Buffalo.

I have just said good-bye to Larry. He seems to want to stop time
as he glances back from the train's first step.

Because he is behind the camera on the cement platform,
my father is not in the picture.

A few seconds after this photograph the train will pull out,
its wailing whistle overpowering our goodbyes.

We will return home, our family of six *five* now.
Nearly the same din and quietude fill our small rented house.

We go about schoolwork and dinners, fights and hugs with the warm
yeastiness of dough rising in a bowl: movement without awareness.

In nine months Larry will be summoned to the Dean's Office,
told that our father has died suddenly of a heart attack, at work.

Larry will be alone when he takes
the evening train home that night to Newburgh.

In thirty-five years Larry, now a doctor, will be summoned
to a hospital in California by his friend, an internist.

He will be the first to hear that our mother has
three tumors in her liver: pancreatic cancer.

The next day our mother will go home from the hospital.
For two weeks friends and relatives will visit, stunned by the news.

Larry, cool to our mother since our father's death,
knows he must return with ardor, now to her bedside.

Soon he will barely leave her house; he spends every day with her
whipping up egg creams and root beer floats, fortifying broth.

Listening to tapes of Jewish songs from her childhood,
the two of them will talk into the night.

In a few weeks he will spoon her ice chips,
buy anything to make her comfortable—

diapers, soothing lotion, an intercom
when she calls wanly from the bedroom.

Always so stylish, our mother looks ancient,
her hair white and flat, skin translucent.

Occasionally she will moan in her sleep, but when awake
Larry will be at her side.

At moments she has a girlish bloom on her face
as if reunited with her first boyfriend.

Larry's three siblings—Elliot, Nancy, myself—look on,
sometimes from the door frame.

We try not to feel disheartened,
not to feel swooped in on.

Putting aside our churlishness
we know his presence is what our mother wants.

Thirty-one days after he is summoned by the internist
Larry will order thirty-one white roses for her casket.

They will drape the dark polished wood
like a white satin dress.

Graveside

IT IS BOTH Father's Day and the last day of a family reunion in the Catskill Mountains, an hour's drive from Newburgh, New York. My brothers and I are making this first visit together to our father's grave, thirty years since his burial in the spring of 1959.

We live three thousand miles away now, a result of our mother's re-marriage eleven months after our father's death, and our own moves to West Virginia, North Carolina, and then to California. Nobody we know, not even a distant relative, lives in Newburgh any more.

The cemetery is not easy to find. First we see the Italian grave-yard, the D'Angelos and the Crosettas, then the Jewish one, then finally our father's grey stone with the line from Pasternak: "To live on in our hearts is not to die." It seems fitting that the stone is so simple—that strangely, it even seems kind, the color of air.

There are twelve small smooth stones that our mother had left on top of the gravestone during her visit before the reunion. Four for his children, eight for the grandchildren he never knew. He hardly had years to know *us* in our growing, our modifying, our tempering or in-ability to temper. The youngest of us, my sister Nancy, was four when he died.

She is in her mid-thirties now and had visited his grave for the first time a few months before we did. We miss her on this pilgrimage, but at least have her directions on how to find his gravestone.

The site had been so difficult for her to locate that after an hour's looking, after climbing over a locked gate and even crawling through a tall hedge, all she could cry out was, "Where *are* you?"

She finally found his grave after walking up and down the rows of stones and brushing off the dried grass that had covered his name, *Benjamin Morris Krames*.

My two brothers and I bring flowers and plants to place against the stone. Red geraniums, hot pink carnations, and gold daisies to drink the grey air. They will die in a few days—we know that—but we need a fervent marker for a memory so buoyant, although his grave, that strange symbol of reality for those remembering, had for so many years lain three thousand miles from our lives.

We put the flowers down and stare quietly, lost in thoughts of how we missed him, how much we had missed all these years. Leaving his grave almost an hour later is difficult, as if his magnetic field surrounds us, permeating all memory. It had taken us so many years to get there together, how could we leave now?

Walking back to the car, I think to myself that with our father's death some fleshing out of his children had stopped: the emotional fine-tuning that can happen from knowing one's parents a very long time, from viewing their eccentricities and occasional grace, from changing in ways they need us to change, growing old after they grow old.

From being with them rather than remembering them.

Somehow we lack the acceptance of each other that our father might have inspired. This man who could calm an argument with a hand clasp or a few words or a well-placed joke might have helped us view each other more tolerantly, more calmly.

We walk fine as a family of adults, and there's a patina of ease among us. But we know the held-at-bay hurt that can erupt like a terrible scald. This sort of injury can occur between any siblings, fatherless or not, but we feel the absence of that parent-cohered bond we might have had had he lived past forty-four. Still, even as the baby among us will soon pass the age our father was when he died, we try—at times we earnestly try—to dispense balm to one other, in his honor.

The Arc of a Single Shooting Star

ELLIOT HAS AN artificial eye.

Late summer 1954, when Elliot was ten and I was five, he had seen a movie about a miner. This detail comes from my older brother Larry; Elliot does not remember seeing such a movie. If Larry is correct, the miner was prospecting for gold and hitting rocks with a pickaxe, which was thrilling to Elliot. Our family lived in Westbury, Long Island, and the next day when Elliot and his best friend Sidney, who lived across the street, were playing, they pretended to be miners. They were having fun hitting rocks with hammers.

A tiny sliver of rock flew into Elliot's right eye. He felt no pain but suddenly saw stars and black spots. At this moment my mother and I were having coffee and cake with Aunt Ida, my mother's first cousin though we called her Aunt Ida. She lived in Levittown, several miles away. The concerned telephone call came from Bernice Feldman, Sidney's mother and my mother's best friend.

My mother gulped a last sip of coffee as we hastily kissed Aunt Ida goodbye, got in the car and sped home. My mother, thirty-two, was seven months pregnant with her fourth child, a daughter who would soon become my sister Nancy. There were no seatbelts then and I sat next to her, trying to thread my hand though the tight angle of her arm on the steering wheel. I liked the sweet smell of her hair, of the Aqua-Net hairspray, but this is also my first memory of feeling scared.

It was mid-afternoon so my father was at work at the die-cutting factory in New York City. My mother assessed the situation and called the doctor, our trusted GP, who said to bring Elliot in immediately. I stayed at home with Larry, thirteen. The GP had no special eye diagnostic equipment in his office, probably just an ophthalmoscope. These were the days before families had ready access to specialists like ophthalmologists. The GP looked at Elliot's eye, cleaned it up a bit, said he'd be fine and sent him home. He did not realize Elliot's retina had been severely damaged.

My brother woke in the middle of the night screaming in pain. My parents called the doctor who had seen my brother earlier that day. Awakened from sleep, the GP said to take him to an eye doctor in the morning, and gave them the name of one. In the 1950s, 911 calls and nighttime ambulances were not assumed parts of a parent's repertoire. The next morning, the ophthalmologist, whose office was across the street from the hospital, had the proper equipment to examine Elliot's eye. Immediately recognizing the dire situation, he gave Elliot an intra-muscular injection of morphine, lifted him up in his arms and carried him across the street to Long Island Jewish Hospital. Together with my mother, they probably ran.

Elliot thought the doctors at the hospital would just be cleaning up the pus forming around his eye; perhaps they would remove the rock sliver. The morphine was easing the pain and making him sleepy.

By the time both of my parents were at the hospital and had conferred with the eye specialists, they had to make the dreadful decision to have Elliot's right eye removed. It was that, or have Elliot go blind because the optic nerve would cause him to lose sight in his left eye, too. Or the most terrifying news—Elliot could die from a virulent brain infection if they did not operate immediately. Up until this moment my parents had never heard of the term for the removal of an eye: enucleation. They could not have conceived that their son would be losing one of his sapphire-blue eyes.

Elliot remembers three doctors with white masks hovering over him, and the large overhead operating-room lights. He remembers somehow waking up mid-operation and feeling no pain. Years later, Elliot would become an anesthesiologist.

During his month-long recovery at the hospital, my mother stayed with him night and day. I missed her terribly and wished I, too, could have an accident so my mother would remain by my side. Years later she told me that she cried so much during that terrible month that when Nancy was born two months later she was amazed the baby wasn't deformed. Elliot's primary memory of the hospital stay is that he became friends with a little girl on the same floor who had leukemia. They played together in the hallway and then one day she was not there because she had died.

From all these details floats a family story that possibly never happened:

> When Elliot was so frail and frightened in those first days after surgery, Rosemary Clooney, who just happened to be at Long Island Jewish Hospital that day—or was it the McGuire Sisters or one of the Andrews Sisters or simply some compassionate nurse?—went to his room and sang a song from *The Pajama Game*, "Hey There." Somehow the singer (or singers) had heard about this poor little boy who had recently lost an eye, asked what room he was in, and then sang him that entire emotional song, "Hey there, you with the stars in your eyes…" The song had been recorded that year, 1954, by Rosemary Clooney and was a huge hit. Larry's memory is that all of us in the family crooned that song to Elliot when he came *home* from the hospital. Elliot has no memory at all of that song being sung to him. Today when I hear that song I begin to cry.

When Elliot's eye was removed, a prosthetic ball was put in place but he would not get an artificial eye for six months. That's how long the orb needed to heal before it could accept a prosthesis. After his bandages were removed he wore an eye patch for six months, like a small pirate.

When Elliot returned to school, he, who by temperament had been fearless, was for the first time self-conscious. Fellow fifth-graders at Bowling Green Elementary School probably had not seen other children with serious injuries, and they would stare or, worse, taunt him. Elliot would not respond by walking away but by saying, "What are you looking at?" and pick a fight, sometimes punching a boy in the face. When he was nearby, Larry would try to stop the fight.

Finally Elliot went with our mother to New York City to see an ocular prosthetist whose office smelled of antiseptic. The prosthetist went to a cabinet and pulled out trays and trays of glass eyes—for him, the blue-eyed ones. This was years before prosthetic eyes were made of acrylic, or formed to the eye socket and adjusted for comfort.

Every year while he was still growing, Elliot would get a new eye. Eventually he would get a new one every five years, and to date has had sixteen right eyes. But no matter how well made the artificial eye is, his right eye is 100% of the time painful. Either it is inflamed or dripping or dry. It is still like seeing stars: less distracting and vivid than when the accident occurred in 1954, but the discomfort is there.

Many years later when Elliot's second wife told him to get help for what she labeled anger management, the psychiatrist, after hearing Elliot's life story, declared that when Elliot lost his eye at ten and then lost his father five years later—in fact, one day before his fifteenth birthday—he never got over being angry.

Elliot, now a world-famous pain doctor and skilled caregiver, does not agree with that psychiatrist's assessment. After all, who can precisely explain even one's own actions and reactions? He acknowledges, however, his volatility, his often pyrotechnic emotions. He knows he ignites with indignation one second and then can completely de-charge the next. We who love him wonder at his equal traits of instant anger and notable sweetness.

He is both extremes and to witness them can be haunting, like the burst, and then graceful and beautiful arc, of a shooting star. For me, watching Elliot erupt, then release, can be like watching over and over again the opposite trajectory of that seemingly harmless, but then horrifying, rock sliver.

The Knitter

MY MOTHER WAS a natural knitter the way someone can be a natural cook. She could knit patterns while watching television or a movie. When my mother went to see "Casablanca" she brought her work with her and knit the entire back of a coat.

She would call herself Madame Defarge, the character who encoded in her knitting the people she chose to have killed. I don't think my mother intended the French Revolution reference, or understood that this double was an angel of death. In any case, she never could have foretold the heartaches that would blanket so much of her life.

At fourteen she was an orphan, her father dying when she was nine, her mother five years later, of pancreatic cancer. She met my father at fifteen, married him at seventeen, became a mother at eighteen, and was widowed with four children at thirty-six, with no savings or insurance policy. Her sister Ray battled depression most of her life and committed suicide. Her brother Willie had a drinking problem and some form of mental illness; no one knew exactly what. Years later he vanished as an adult. No one knows why, or even when. In all, my mother had three husbands, the middle one a very bad mistake. One week after her seventy-first birthday, she was diagnosed with pancreatic cancer. She understood the prognosis and one month later we attended her funeral.

In telling my mother's life it is easy to emphasize the grief, the fraying. But I remember her as a force of nature. Irrepressible Irene, talking and laughing, drinking coffee, smoking, cooking Italian dishes she learned from her first landlady, being angry a lot and prone to screaming, and loving my father very much but being upset by his fatigue. Cardiology was young then and my father's faulty valve was not replaced.

Other indelible memories: working when other mothers didn't, being a fabulous dancer, coloring her hair blond and looking like Marilyn Monroe, enjoying a Perfect Rob Roy, a scotch with small but equal parts sweet and dry vermouth (her final license plate was PRRBRY, as in PeRfect RoB RoY), and loving me, totally.

And knitting. Most women of her generation knitted, but she, who had dreamed of becoming a textile designer yet never graduated from high school, took knitting to a different orbit. She knitted hundreds of sweaters, a slew of afghans, several coats and vests, a few svelte dresses, and countless baby booties and blankets, socks, slippers, mittens, and vests. I think she dreamed in yarn.

Until I was twelve, my mother knit every sweater I owned. Then I bought a Villager cardigan: $13.00, or twenty-six hours of babysitting. Still, I reveled in those sweaters she created. I especially loved my scarlet cable knit cardigan with mother-of-pearl buttons. Also a lilac bolero. No buttons, and little daisies embroidered in white and yellow angora near the collar.

She even owned two knitting stores. The first, in Brooklyn, opened before I was born, was called Irene's Yarn Studio, like some glamorous Hollywood gig although it was in Bensonhurst, a decidedly blue-collar area of Brooklyn. She opened the second store after we'd moved from Long Island and gone "upstate" to Newburgh. She named this store The Yarn Mart, three syllables that seemed to command, "Buy my yarn."

For a year she would take weekly drives to Bear Mountain, teach an evening class of knitting to cadets at West Point to help them learn to relax. This was the mid-1950s when teaching young men, especially future Cold War army generals, something like knitting as a method of relaxation was practically unheard of. It probably still is.

My sister and I spent many childhood hours with our arms held out about a foot apart, fingers together and vertical. Mom would open up a loose skein of yarn and drape it over our outstretched arms. Then she would take a thread of wool and wrap it with her right hand around her own outstretched left hand, winding it into a soft ball from which she would then knit a garment or afghan. I enjoyed the still-faint sheep smell of the worsted wool.

My mother knitted every day. Either her hands were engaged in an item to keep herself or a loved one warm, or she was contemplating her next intricate creation. Mom was an avid reader and would take fat novels to bed with her, but in daylight she would read books of knitting patterns.

When I think of the next stage, I think of her *counting* (...*five, six, seven, eight...*) and going on something like autopilot. She'd get almost beady-eyed as she'd read a pattern, trying to commit it to memory. Then she'd start clicking those needles and flicking that yarn, counting silently (though I could discern the numbers on her lips) until she got the hang of the pattern. She'd pause for a deep breath, then count some more. After all, knitting—whether stockinet stitch, garter stitch, ribbing, cables, or some other elaboration on knit and purl—is arithmetic.

And it is caring, for the generous intent of hands can be felt in the warmth of a nubby wrap-around scarf or perfectly fitted woolen gloves or a thick Fisherman's Knit pullover.

My mother, though a generous knitter, was not a patient teacher to me. She would exclaim with genuine puzzlement, "I don't understand why you're not good at this!" So I never really learned to knit, or to feel comfortable knitting. Without meaning to, she set the bar too high. She was too attuned to yarn and I was too halting, dropped too many stitches, kept on forgetting how to cast on. I did not share her talents with wool, which disappointed her and defeated me.

Now, however, my daughter is learning to knit. She wishes she had gotten to know her grandmother better before she died at a young seventy-one, hadn't been slightly afraid of her and had learned to knit from Nana. But in *her* knitting she can feel my mother, see her through each knit-and-purl outcome, and somehow forgive my mother's impatience or the few times she yelled at her. Slowly my daughter is learning to add and decrease and bind off stitches. She understands that knitting is a work of love in progress.

My own daughter will never refer to herself as Madame Defarge but seems to be echoing her grandmother, almost as if she is picking up a dropped stitch with a skipped generation of skill.

The Floor Froze

I STRADDLED MY stepfather's shoulders as he waded through December snow, blue-white in the moonlight. Snow came to his waist, and my feet, as we moved from the paved road to the West Virginia log cabin where five of us were living when I was eleven. My stepfather stormed the snow-drifted door and we entered our two-room house, the coal stove stone-quiet. My nose constricted and the air smelled like a freezer. But the greatest surprise: the floor was crunchy. Moisture in the linoleum, never apparent in summer when it made the floor quiet and supple, had frozen, and it seemed we were walking on sugar. We walked through the kitchen to the one bedroom where five of us slept, white chenille bedspreads spread out like snow. Getting on with the business of the night, my stepfather stoked that resistant coal stove while the four of us turned to bed for warmth. Tamped down next to my young sister, our single bed gave no reassurances. Certain I would freeze by morning, I accepted no comfort from my mother, thought even my tears would freeze. Then, when that tardy stove glowed— red-black in the dark—sleep brought its own blanket.

Sleeping with My Mother

At times when I was nine and fifteen
I loved to sleep with my mother,
benefiting from those crevices of time,
first when she was widowed, and later divorced.
I would fall asleep next to her, smiling,
having shifted our bodies
until we both rested comfortably,
regaining that compromise
we must have formed in her pregnancy.

I missed sleeping with her as an adult
but I did sleep with my mother
two weeks before she died
and when I slept with her that night
I knew her body had missed me.

My arms encircled her waist
though by this time the cancer
had ballooned her stomach.
I held her as we shifted our positions, and
as my palm homed to its familiar place around
her and rested there, it was she
who smiled as we drifted off to sleep.
I knew this
though she faced away from me.

As If These Toes

More than any other part of my body
my feet are my mother's
the way they splay broadly
where the foot bouquets into toes.

Three days before my mother died
Alexandra painted my toenails fuchsia,
the pink of the bougainvillaea
flanking a house my mother used to live in.

Alexandra gave my mother a pedicure too
but only clipped the horny tip of the nail,
leaving the toes rounded,
clean and buff-colored
for the crossover to death.

Every month for ten years
my mother drove to a nail salon
then returned home with all her nails
a shocking pink or coral or vermilion.
Now she was dying in a rented hospital bed,
her nails as unadorned as flesh.

I massaged her feet that last week
when talk of the future
stopped us
the sickness leaving little to do
but rub the rose-scented lotion
over the balls of her feet.

One month after my mother's death
my pink nail polish has cracked and chipped
and I look at these toes as if they could transport me back
to her embrace, her morning phone calls
her greetings "Angel face" and "Love of my life."
Even her withering
"you aren't you didn't you should have"
are part of that body I long for.

My Mother's Mattress

This mattress felt four husbands
my mother's three, my own,
so many children's bodies
and countless floating sheets.

I feel my mother
in long and spatial ways.
So many decades ago I slept within her
as she slept on this mattress.
I can even sleep on her sleep with my father
all those years before I was born.

We have same and different memories
of moves (through states and men)
mixed inside the ticking and horsehair,
firm yet flat the way mattresses are no longer made.
Occasionally a thick horsehair will thorn out of the stripes
right through the white sheets.

When I say to her "You don't know me"
and she returns "You're not the daughter I used to know"
we both hold to false recriminations:
our love a depth charge.
Mothers and daughters know each other in their bones.
With my own daughter
there is hurt and healing and helping and holding beyond words.

The mattress is now supplanted
with a higher, more pillowy one.
You are gone eighteen years,
the knowledge we had I search for/cannot
replace.

Summer Heat

summer burns
but this annealing summer
put us through fires that
cracked and crazed
this large family
this collection of vessels

even the tacky
dampness
of summer air
does not deplete
the way streams
of tears
or spitted words
have left our hearts
so flagged in August

The Heartwork of O. Henry
for my brother Elliot

Sibling love is a gift like no other,
so already *there*:
all that DNA,
memories, shared laughter, common fears.
Even our parents' hair is dealt to us, like playing cards,
in just a few combinations of color, waviness and texture.
Their eyes become ours with only a few Mendelian possibilities.

Yet veils of mistrust can cloud
looks between brothers and sisters.
Childhood words of attack still rive like a knife,
silence and detachment cut as closely.

Determining the location of our mother's seventieth birthday party
might seem small, but for you and me
it was not.
I had wanted it at my house.
You made it clear it should be at yours.
That light dust of hurt siblings know all too well
threatening to fall, again,
so when you called to say
"No party is more important than your feelings,
let's have the party at your house,"
I had already imagined luscious pink roses on your glass dining room table,
a dozen champagne flutes bubbling as we sat down to eat—
and you had imagined my long maple table covered with a tablecloth,
laden with food as we toasted our mother.

The party was at my house,
a happy memory.
Now we know she would have only one more birthday.

In the O. Henry short story, "The Gift of the Magi,"
the young wife with no money cuts her long hair and sells it
to buy her husband a watch chain for Christmas
while at the same time he sells his watch and buys her
a tortoise-shell comb to embrace her lustrous hair.

Your call was the gift then, nineteen years ago,
and as I remember it now,
the heartwork of O. Henry,
our own story.

Former Sister-in-Law

At the intersection
you do not see me.

But I see you
cool and elegant as ever
your arm on a different husband
my brother no longer your walking partner.

Walking past, I recall the instant
you arrived at the hospital
just twenty minutes before
my son was born
and somehow, in the fluid movement of that room
my head rested on your lap during all those pushes,
especially the last one
when exclamations filled the room.
Your face glows in the photograph
of that moment
your jubilation clear.

Now, when our paths cross
but do not cross
I am relieved you do not see me
and we need not fumble for words.

Double Mocha

for my sister Nancy

across the outdoor café table I grasp
your hand
our other hands
around glassed double mochas

white drowsy milkiness
infusing
sweet chocolate tawny
darkening
bitter jolt espresso
deepening
layered burnt sienna

our love resembles
those floating layers
surface tension barely intact
the lighter color lifting the darker
the heat
finding its balance

we cannot harden to each other
our words a supple wave

always believing
in the existence of a shore

Lanolin, or What Sisters Do

FOR THIRTEEN YEARS, from 1994 to 2007, my sister Nancy owned a deli in Ithaca, New York. *Sadie D's,* named after her dachshund Sadie, the "D" a compression of Dachshund and Deli Café. Sadie herself was quite a coffee hound, slurping down her own fair share of cups of coffee. New York state health regulations kept her out of her eponymous deli, but Sadie would finish just about every cup of coffee my sister drank at home.

One time Sadie D's sponsored a contest to guess how many dachshund images had been collected in the deli by Nancy or donated by customers, because Sadie D's truly was a dachshund deli, with an almost endless array of practical as well as silly items in that comical hot-dog shape. There were ceramic figurines, salt and pepper shakers, Slinky toys, serving bowls, bookends, mugs, plumber's levelers, horizontal thermometers—you name it—plus paintings, drawings, and photos galore. Mike Lane, an Ithaca Common Council member, won the contest by guessing 1,450. In total there were almost 1,500 dachshund items. He won a $50 gift certificate, which he used for five lunches: his usual— a ham-and-cheese sandwich, a bag of Wise potato chips, and a Dr. Pepper.

The deli was famous for its kitschy dog décor, but mostly it was famous for my sister's friendliness. Along with every sandwich she meticulously made or steaming cup of coffee she prepared came a big smile and earnest question about how a kid was faring in college, how a dad was doing after his latest round of chemo, or how an accounting practice was holding up during tough economic times. Almost always, even during Ithaca's long and dreary winters, she would wear her beloved San Francisco Giants baseball cap that kept her soft curly brown hair in place. The rest of her deli uniform, in addition to a crisp apron, consisted of hi-top sneakers, blue jeans, a washed but not ironed button-down shirt, suspenders, and earrings with a food or dachshund motif that set off her blue-green eyes.

Sadie D's *was* famous; it's gone now. After thirteen years the place pretty much just closed one day, unable to cover expenses as gas prices rose and the price of trucking food rose with it. The clientele in an economically depressed town in central New York, despite the august presence of Cornell, couldn't pay enough to keep up with soaring costs of roast beef or pastrami, half-sour pickles, coffee beans or tomatoes.

But really, the restaurant went bankrupt because of grief. Like Alice's Restaurant in the movie of that title, someone could have posted a sign in the window of Sadie D's: "This restaurant is closed on account of too much dying."

Nancy's son Josh worked in the deli, blending up egg salad and tuna salad and serving customers most days after high school. He was still working out the gawkiness of those late teenage years, the planes of his face not having quite found their home. Rail thin, with a haircut trying to keep his curly dark blond hair under control, he too was famous for his Sadie D's smile. His particular pleasure was making a Godfather—freshly sliced Genoa salami, capicola, mortadella, two slices of provolone, garlic red peppers, and a house-made Italian dressing that he blended in the Cuisinart and nicknamed the *l-o-o-o-o-v-e* dressing.

Serving customers gave Josh such satisfaction that he was considering enrolling in culinary school after graduation. One afternoon, after eating lunch at a local pizza parlor with two friends, he was a front-seat passenger in a car going around a turn too fast. The driver, Josh's friend Matt, was killed instantly when the car hit a tree. The EMTs who found Josh tried to revive him, but his neck was broken and he'd sustained massive internal injuries. Three hours later, Nancy and her husband Natan had to decide to take Josh off life support. This was early evening, May 13, 2003, three days before his nineteenth birthday.

Their daughter Rachel was living near me in San Francisco, attending college. Her dad had called her with the horrifying news, but at that hour Josh was still alive. When Rachel came over to my house, where my family had begun to congregate as families do when terrible news has broken, Rachel opened the door with a hopeful face: perhaps a miracle had happened and Josh had improved. By then I had gotten the second call from Natan. When Rachel was inside my kitchen I told her Josh had died. Her knees buckled and I protected her from hitting her head on the kitchen counter as she collapsed into my arms.

The year after Josh died, in a miasma of grief and in an attempt to regain purpose in her life, Nancy trained to become a fire fighter and EMT. Two years into this volunteer job, one that she did off hours while running Sadie D's, she ruptured two discs while responding with other fire fighters to a rural house on fire. Nancy was trying to rescue a scared dog running from the house and she slipped on black ice. During her six-week recovery from back surgery, she couldn't find capable employees to take her place at the deli. One of the boys she entrusted with running the deli stole money from the cash register. This was a boy she had taken under her wing after Josh died.

Several years before Josh's death, I spent two weeks with Nancy and her family in Ithaca. I have a repetitive strain injury in my arms, and when I was in my most acute pain and on medical leave from work, I sought my sister's help. I sought her nearness. At night, at her home during dinner, she would cut my food for me. During the day I would stay with her at Sadie D's, reading the newspaper or trolling through issues of *People* and appreciating the perfect sandwiches and cups of tea she would make for me.

But mostly I would sit not far from the counter and gaze at her, watch her slice pounds of tomatoes or a bucket of pickles and feel something like awe. My arms were gimpy and she could wield a knife with ease. Her small but sinewy hands were commanding and dexterous, though they seemed dry, chapped from the harsh winters or from having her hands in water so much of the workday. I wanted to take her hands in mine, warm them, massage them with soothing lotion. Still, I would marvel at the way those hands could fly, how she choreographed the sandwich counter, espresso machine, dishwasher, telephone, and cash register, all the while dispensing food and drink with that sweet tomboy cheer her customers relished.

When I would sit in the rectangle of her deli I would especially appreciate the moments when there were no customers. Then I would go on a reverie, remembering the two of us in her crib.

In late November 1954, when I was five, Nancy was born. Even though I had two older brothers whom I loved and parents I truly loved, Nancy was a connection I had never known before. She was a sister, and she was bliss.

Not even six pounds when she was born, she became my tiny roommate with my twin bed against one wall and her crib against the other. She was my mother's fourth child, so when Nancy would wail my mother would often let her cry herself to sleep. I could not believe such meanness! I would start crying, too, not accepting my mother's assurances that the baby was not going to die and that sometimes babies needed to cry.

I would close the bedroom door and quietly climb inside her crib, lie down next to her, whisper shushing sounds and sing "Rock-a-Bye Baby" or "Raisins and Almonds," the two lullabies I knew. I would stroke her cheek and breathe in the sweet scent of Johnson's baby lotion that my mother had rubbed on her face and neck. The gentle perfume would mix with the strong, healing scent of Desitin, diaper rash cream my mother would spread on Nancy's bottom, and to this day Desitin is one my favorite smells.

It was just the two of us, and I was saving her.

Nearly fifty years later, while observing Nancy at Sadie D's when it was I who was helpless (and often silently crying), she was saving me. Those late afternoons, like an energetic yet benevolent queen, she had dominion over her deli, feeding me bountiful sandwiches, buoying me with folk music on the sound system, making the place clean and comforting, and sometimes coming around the counter and giving me a kiss on the cheek.

This covenant of soothing continues. Now after Josh's death, there are so many days when I do my best, again, to calm her. In both of our lives, many problems but also many resolutions continue to rise; talking about them is a great gift of the day. We also talk about simpler things, like salad dressing and what we cooked for dinner last night, whether we're happy with our most recent haircut—usually we're not—and the latest hilarious thing that June, her four-year-old granddaughter, has said.

Nancy and I live on opposite coasts and are separated by states and time zones but when we speak it is as if we are in the same room, hermetically sealed, sort of like being back in her deli or even back in that crib. We try to laugh and to make each other laugh, and often this is so as not to cry. This is what sisters do, or at least this is what we do, and it is so much more than the work of our hands. Companionship and comforting and our easy ability to talk to each other: these are our emollients, our sisters' lanolin.

The Feeling of Hands
for Michael Lavigne

Sometimes I can feel the slight hesitation or surprise
when I say to guests, "At our home
we hold hands before eating." I grasp the hand
of the person to my left and to my right.
Sometimes I reach across if only three of us are around
the kitchen table and say words of welcome.
"Let your hands tie a knot across the table,"
that line from "Follow" sung by Richie Havens, floats through my mind.

If there are more guests and we sit around the dining room table
sometimes a few have already lit into their baked chicken
or mashed potatoes with a sunny dollop of butter
or requested the salt and pepper shakers and I say,
"Can we all hold hands?"

It's the holding of hands, this necklace of palms,
that I like even more than the words of reflection.
I grab my husband's hand or my son's or daughter's
or someone to my left or right whose grip
I would not otherwise feel, and think
I can never get enough of this warm hand.
I want this hand in mine. I feel the palm creamy smooth
or unexpectedly grainy or sense the sheen of tender skin.

From 1961 to 1966 in Greensboro, North Carolina,
I would often sit around the Bernstein family table.
Susan, the oldest child, was my best friend.
A Jewish family with six children and not even Orthodox,
Shirley and Martin Bernstein owned a sprawling old house
on many acres named Justamere Farm.
In those years of the 1960s this was the greatest table I thought,
respite from my mother and stepfather's fighting
or stony silences, tension that made it hard to enjoy
the food in front of me.

As often as I could gain invitation I would be the ninth
seated in the Bernstein dining room. The immense round table
would be covered with a white tablecloth, or sometimes plaid,
and laden with pot roast and gravy with slowly roasted potatoes
or mounds of fried chicken accompanied by ears of corn
and peas and carrots. And many glasses of milk.
A cook would go around the table and serve us,
an experience that always surprised me but she too
seemed pleased to be in the company of this family.

Then the nine of us, if all six children were present,
would hold hands around the circle of table
and Mr. Bernstein would say words of welcome
and gratitude in his southern accent.
He owned a chain of jewelry stores
and was president of an organization of Christians and Jews.
Mrs. Bernstein was the leader of my Girl Scout troop
and in 1963 ours was the first in North Carolina to integrate.
This was her firm resolve.
She had the deeper accent and I loved her voice too
but when Mr. Bernstein spoke before dinner
he sounded so sturdy and trustworthy
so melodious with his comforting words
and the hands of the Bernstein child to my left and to my right
felt so comfortable in mine that I thought
If I am ever lucky enough to marry
and have children and serve dinner,
which I was sure I never would be,
I will keep this tradition no matter where I live.

Even then I loved that knotted chain,
the heated contours, magnetic field of skin.

The Rich Scent of Pine-Sol

A BOTTLE OF Pine-Sol costs a few dollars. Almost everyone can afford Pine-Sol, but for me that cleaner carries the scent of wealth.

I still associate that *I've-cleaned-your-house* scent with affluence because of Ella, housekeeper of my best friend in elementary school, Lois Shapiro. Ella cleaned the Shapiro house daily, it seemed, with Pine-Sol. In the late 1950s, I would occasionally go home after school with Lois who lived in the wealthy section of Newburgh (her father was a doctor). We would jump off the school bus, walk in the side door of her house into the big kitchen, and I would smell the unapologetic scent of Pine-Sol. My cheer would turn to envy.

Lois was too lucky to have a spic-and-span house to come home to; to have a housekeeper clean it every day. I cared about such things, because at nine I loved a clean house almost more than anything. I was the housecleaner in my house: the Krames family Cinderella I sometimes thought. Both of my parents worked and it was my job to clean the house when I got home from school. My brothers didn't help because it was the 1950s and boys didn't do housework then. My sister had just turned four.

I would step off the school bus, walk to my house, and begin chores. Make the beds, Ajax the bathroom, fold laundry, polish furniture and, a few times a week, vacuum. Most days I would also start dinner, calling my mother's knitting store—JOhn 1–4460—to see what she had in mind for me to cook.

My father worked as a die-cutter in a pocketbook factory. Our family got by on his small salary, plus a little extra from my mother's store. It wasn't that I yearned to be rich—I just want someone else to do the housework.

I dreamed of a housekeeper like Ella, with her hair pulled back in a ponytail, flow-y brown skirt and beige blouse, soft black shoes. I wished that someone like her would enter our rented house after I left it for fourth grade—and with command reach for a bucket underneath the sink, fill it with warm water, put in a few tablespoons of treacle-colored Pine-Sol and watch the golden agent transform water into a milky elixir. Then dip the blue sponge into this liquid, squeeze it carefully and move it up and down the walls, the counter, the stair railing and windowsills, erasing scuff marks and fingerprints, traces of crumbs or dog hair. Then wipe with clear water so as not to leave a film.

My house would sparkle when I opened the door, and as I stepped inside there would be that piney-rich scent of a clean house. I would think I had entered the home of a very lucky—rich—person, and that person would be me, and I would have nothing to do but sit down and do homework.

This Name

ON AUGUST 4, 1949, I am born Jennifer Ann Krames. When I am five, I do not like to wear clothes. There is a New York stripper, Ann Corio, whose name is splashed all over newspaper headlines. My father nicknames me Jennifer Ann Corio Krames and even as a small child I get the joke.

A few years later when I reflect on the name I've been given, the Jennifer part sounds pretty to me, like its forebear Guinevere, but sits askew on young shoulders. It's a big name and there are few Jennifers in the 1950s. Only, it seems, the movie star Jennifer Jones, though I learn when she dies many years later that her real name was Phyllis Isley, her second husband, David O. Selznick, having fabricated one afternoon before they were married the alliterative Jennifer Jones.

As a child I always have to spell my name, emphasize there are two n's, that it does not begin with a G. Sometimes I have to tell people how to pronounce it. My Polish grandfather does his best with Jenevee. Sometimes people call me Jenny, like the grandmother after whom I am named, although she spelled her name J-e-n-n-i-e but much of her life went by her Yiddish name Shaindel.

I am nine. Within a year of my father's death, my mother elopes with Warren Duliere whose name in French means "of the ivy." Hard to pronounce. Hard to spell.

In a few months we move to a tiny town in West Virginia—Capon Bridge—with a two-room elementary school. I skip the sixth grade, learn very little in the seventh, which also includes a brief move to Morgantown, West Virginia, where my mother, stepfather, sister, brother, and I move in with Warren's mother. After a three-month foray to Morgantown, we cannot live any more with my step-grandmother. She hates my mother and draws me aside to tell me, repeatedly.

In the spring when we move to Greensboro, North Carolina, it is as if I have not attended school for two years.

School is not the only thing topsy-turvy in my life, so when I enter the last part of seventh grade and my mother takes me aside outside the principal's office, what she asks will not seem strange. Everything seems up for grabs. She says, "Why don't you just take his name."

I enroll as Jennifer Duliere. The secretary has no idea this is not my name. No birth certificate is required. For five years my friends, teachers, and even my family call me Jennifer Duliere. A boy I like nicknames me Jen Dooley, as in Hang Down Your Head Tom Dooley.

June, 1966. Graduating from Walter Hines Page Senior High School in Greensboro, I stride across the auditorium stage, shaking beneath my cap and gown. The principal hands me my diploma. We lock eyes and he calls out *Jennifer Krames*.

A week before, in his office, I insist that my real name be put on my diploma. This meeting occurs several years before the fierce assertions of the Women's Movement. At sixteen I am a quiet and dutiful student, but know I do not want Duliere on my diploma. A murmur waves over the audience as the strange name, Krames, rings out. Perhaps class-mates are wondering if schoolmarmish Jennifer had a shotgun wedding last night.

I am relieved that tomorrow my now-divorced mother and sister and I will head out in our Vauxhall to drive across country. We will move to San Francisco where we will know no one, and no one will know our names.

In college, in California, the name Jennifer Krames continues to be that comfortable but somewhat loose shawl I wore on high school graduation day. When I marry at twenty-two I cannot feign feminist attachment to my birth name, and I take Futernick, my husband's sur-name. Now I am sixty-two and it seems so many movie stars and singers and even writers are named Jennifer that I will never have to spell my first name again. I often have to spell Futernick, make it clear when I say the letters that the first one is an F like Frank, not S like Sam. Or I have to correct the way people mispronounce it, but that's fine. It's the final one. I plan to die wearing this name.

Heart's Geography

I.
I have an uneasy relationship with trains.

My sister and I escaped on a Pullman
leaving at late dusk, arriving at dawn.
Greensboro to Levittown.
Drunk and furious, my stepfather Warren
had beaten up my mother.
I cannot remember why he acted so crazy.
After all the screaming and blur and terror subsided,
the only words I could spit out were, "You are dirt beneath my feet."
I did not know swear words then.
The evening before we left on the train
Rabbi Asher gave my mother money
for her daughters' rushed departure.
Saying goodbye to our mother we cried and clung to her neck.
I tried to be brave.
I was five years older than Nancy.

My sister has no memory of the violence
the afternoon before we boarded the Pullman train,
shielded perhaps in the blanket
of a seven-year-old's tenacious flu.
To this day she loves trains, that lulling click-clack hum.
She remembers lying safely next to me.
Though I marveled at the fine cotton sheets
of our fevered berth,
I did not sleep that night.

Morning's destination:
Aunt Ida and Uncle Nat's immaculate Levitt house.
Uncle Nat was shocked to see how thin I had become.
For two months that summer
he took me every evening after dinner to the Village Green
and ordered me a chocolate malted.
So I could gain weight, he said.
We would sit in the booth of the soda fountain
as he patiently waited for me to drink
that delicious cold concoction.
Waited an hour at least.
Then I would put my small hand in his,
so warm, so bear-like
as we walked home to Aunt Ida and Nancy.
I gained three pounds the summer I turned thirteen.

II.
"I thought you grew up in a house with a white picket fence,"
a woman once told me, literally meaning a *white picket fence*.
I relished telling her the opposite, in blazing detail,
a danger this telling
but what would that fence indicate, even to her?
Protection as spectral as an x-ray?
A fair rebuttal that there were happy stories, too,
there had to be,
or that I seemed to her
like someone untouched by sorrow?

I have told hard stories of my childhood,
its abandonments and abruptions:
my father's sudden death,
my mother's elopement eleven months later
with Warren, nine years older than my oldest brother;
how five of us lived for five months in a two-room log cabin
in West Virginia and I was not one of three kids
in the seventh grade with indoor plumbing or drinking water;
eating squirrel (which is entirely dark meat) because squirrel
is what Warren often shot for our dinner;
being told by my stepfather's mother that I would get
a brain tumor because I read too much,
or hearing her shrill litany every day of my mother's faults.
The three schools in one semester
and the ten by the time I finished high school.

The death of my beloved Aunt Ray, my mother's sister,
by suicide, an overdose of sleeping pills—
my family driving through the night to the hospital
in New York where she lay in a coma. I was in the eighth grade.
The nurse telling me, "Talk to her, she can probably hear you,"
but I could not locate the right words.

The following night, screaming alongside my mother
as her brother Willie, the bohemian uncle I loved so much,
locked himself and his tall girlfriend Kitty
in the bathroom of Aunt Ray's home.
Willie was punching Kitty, choking her. My stepfather stormed
the bathroom door, pinned Willie to the floor, and as
my mother's hands were trembling she dialed the police.
When they arrived, Willie was straitjacketed and taken to Bellevue.

Another exodus in the night, this time in the tenth grade,
driven by some stranger my mother hired
so she, my sister, and I could escape Warren
and move in, two states away,
with my two brothers attending the same university.

In these stories it is easy to convey my mother
as unhinged or having made poor choices
or not having protected me
but the truth is there's another version:
her love for me so enveloping and unmeasured
it is my only beacon in all these wanderings.
Her love my salvation, for it is the connection that will not vanish.

III.
It is tempting to share sad, shocking, or surprising tales
from one's life, especially one's childhood.
Our hard stops, like pushpins on a map,
stud memory with a painful pleasure, even pride,
yet a tale can be told one way as easily as another.
Memory is a Cat's Cradle.
Flip stories one direction
and they're horizontal
another, vertical
depending on which side we look
or choose to remember.

Shadows and cobwebs darken
so many stories we keep private
even many we choose to share,
overlaying our narrative with a coat of gloom—
a slop bucket hauled out on a ship deck,
intended to be thrown overboard but missing the sea entirely,
soaking instead
the very planks on which we walk.

I no longer wish this moldering—
wish instead to turn to the light,
to phototrope like plants deep within the forest
that grow straight upward
searching for pieces of sun.

Marriage

Go with Bob

Love Tourette's

I have consuming need for my beloved, he knows—
and I hope he is not sorry.
                    —*Kimiko Hahn, "Xenicus Longipes"*

Sometimes it seems like a syndrome—

this build up
needing emancipation—
squeeze of hands, nuzzle, kiss quick or deliciously long—
arms draped around shoulders
saying "I love you,"
"You're the best,"
"You make me happy,"
"I'm lucky."

This need welling up
neurological charge
buzzing overloaded electrical circuit
lovestorm—
turbulence
that cannot be contained
must be shouted   whispered,
revelatory
releasing

like the moon with its gravitational pull, inexorable
cresting wave that cannot remain furled,
impulse finding its way upward
expelled, with such sweetness   such love
then returning to that deep place—
inventory of emotion.

Sometimes the urge surfaces gently
like a blossom   fallen from a tree   over a stream
the current may take it under
quietly   but then it rises   again
stays   floats serenely downstream

or the build up includes doubts
of self   of other
worrisome
in their rising,
bubbling up bringing up sludge
percolation of bewilderment and need,
melancholic bass in one's own large choir

or the urge fires too many times
like a pinball machine in which balls keep popping up.
Still, even metal balls come to rest.

Surely sex carries in it, encoded
not just biological need of procreation
but also
this primal firing,
exclamatory,
needing seeking its own
de-charging through connecting, again and again

relieving distress
not through words but fingertips, fingerprints,
lips
shaping not syllables but other fleshy expression, inchoate
to be completed   continued   perfected perhaps
the next time
and the next.

Alone at night or earliest morning or noon
words for poems come like feelings
like love itself
a gift sometimes astonishing
sometimes unwanted
unbidden yet insistent
always there
rising.

Go with Bob

IN OCTOBER 1969, two years and two months after the Summer of Love, I met the man I would marry at the play *Hair* in San Francisco. Actually, we met two hours before the play.

It was a blind date set up by my mother and the internist she worked for, Alan Abrams. My mother was his receptionist and bookkeeper. As a result of an arcane arrangement, Alan was the doctor called upon to administer to the cast of *Hair*. Because cast members eventually get naked and rock out in close proximity with one another, the entire company came down with an upper respiratory-tract infection during Previews Week.

Opening night was threatened and Dr. Abrams was summoned. He listened to their hearts, peered in their throats, and gave them antibiotics. He took my mother along to offer strength in numbers or perhaps out of a sense of generosity. She wasn't a nurse but she was a mother, so she knew how to take their temperatures and, being a Jewish mother and something of a free spirit herself, she probably gave them hugs. This could have been a scene from *Hair*.

As payment, Alan declined money and asked for ten tickets. He took six and gave my mother four. Alan earmarked five tickets for the Abrams family—himself, his wife and three kids—and saved the sixth one to invite Bob Futernick, son of his best friend Joe, to attend the play on Friday night, October 17.

On Wednesday before that Friday, Alan called Bob's parents' house in Menlo Park and found to his delight that Bob was in the Bay Area, visiting for several days. Alan asked if Bob could stay until Friday to see the play and Bob agreed. At the time he was living in Squaw Valley as a soon-to-be ski bum (it hadn't snowed yet) but he *was* working, earning $47.00 a week doing specialty hand bookbinding for his father's commercial bindery, Foster and Futernick Co., in San Francisco. Bob had to be back in Squaw Valley to work at his binding studio no later than

Saturday morning. He had to complete the repair of a bible needed for a client's wedding.

The year before, 1968, Bob had been experiencing lingering effects from a ski accident and when he was in the Bay Area he would see Alan as his doctor. Whenever he did, my mother would peer at him and say, "Robert, I have a girl for you. My daughter Jennifer. She has a boyfriend, Steve, but I don't like him." Steve was a tall, smart, good-looking Jewish medical student and she still didn't like him.

On the same Wednesday that Alan called Bob, my mother told me she had four tickets to *Hair* and wanted to take my sister and me. I asked her to let me take Steve with the fourth ticket. Steve and I were back together again and I thought this might be just the thing to re-ingratiate him with my mother. However, when he heard my mother would be there he declined the invitation. With that fourth ticket she invited a guy she was dating named Jim.

On the Friday morning of the play, my mother informed me that Bob Futernick would be going—sort of as my date—and that I would really like him because he was handsome and adorable. I knew I wouldn't because a guy my mother thought was handsome and adorable couldn't be.

Alan and Barbara Abrams invited us for dinner, pre-play, at their house on Jackson Street, not far from where *Hair* was playing at the Curran Theatre. My mother, Jim, my fourteen-year-old sister Nancy, and I entered their large brick house and walked through the hallway to the family room where the other playgoers had already congregated.

I saw Bob Futernick talking to one of the Abrams kids. I noticed his shoulder-length wavy black hair, very handsome face, the stylish brown loafers he was wearing (borrowed from his brother Ken, I later learned), and the unexpected aura of kindness he exuded. I thought, "Oh shit. My mother is right!" The next second I had a vision: *I'm going to marry him.*

We hadn't met yet, but there was an eagerness to talk and listen that he telegraphed—this sweetness, this open-heartedness—that was precisely what I was seeking.

I sat next to Bob at dinner and also at the play. When the musical came to its exuberant finale, "Let the Sunshine In," the audience was invited onstage to dance along with cast members. Not everyone in the audience joined in, but Bob, Nancy, and I looked at each other, thought *why not* and went up and danced to that pulsating anthem of happiness. Soon it was just those four exhortative words—let the sunshine in—playing over and over to that infectious beat. And the three of us rocking out on stage with a whole lot of other people.

Afterward our group of ten walked up Geary Street to parked cars. My mother asked, "Jennifer, how are you getting back to Berkeley?" I was a senior at Cal, also working fifteen hours a week as a clerk at Lucas Books near campus. Like Bob, I had to work the next day.

Bob told my mother he was driving back to Squaw Valley and could take me home since it was on his way. Riding over the Bay Bridge in his sleek blue Porsche was quietly romantic, and I was drawn to the charm of this bookbinder-skier. However, I knew I would be seeing my off-again, on-again boyfriend Steve the next night, and as Bob and I talked in the car I alluded to the fact that I was dating someone.

We reached Berkeley and Bob pulled up in front of my apartment. I wasn't ready to say goodbye and asked if he would like to see the art posters I'd gotten in Israel the previous summer.

When Bob and I entered the apartment the light was on. My roommate Wendie was there. Normally she spent weekends at her boyfriend's apartment but she had a fever and had decided to sleep in her own bed that night. Bob and I peeked into the bedroom to say hello. The two of them chatted and I showed Bob the posters.

I then gave him a chaste hug at the door and told him to stop by sometime. This was the man I sensed I was going to marry, but I did not have his address or telephone number and I did not give him mine. Inexplicably, it did not seem right to exchange this information.

I saw Steve on Saturday night and by Sunday morning we'd had a whopper of a fight. I was only twenty but felt my romantic life was over. By Sunday afternoon I was sobbing to Wendie.

"What should I *do-o-o*? I'm the worst cliché. I can't live with him and I can't live without him."

By now Wendie was pretty sick of Steve. "Why don't you call that guy Bob? He seemed really nice."

"Wow, that's a good idea. *I will*," I answered, drying my tears.

I resolved to invite Bob to Berkeley so I could talk to him about the problems in my love life. This was selfish (I knew that) but figured it was better to be truthful, and besides, I sensed Bob might have some suggestions for dealing with Steve, a difficult boyfriend I was still pining for.

I called my mother to get Alan Abrams' home phone number and gave her the briefest outline of what had transpired. She was delighted I wanted to follow up with Bob. I then called Dr. Abrams. After a few niceties I was feeling weepy again over my heartache, yet still managed to ask Dr. Abrams how to reach Bob. He wasn't surprised I wanted to call Bob but he was no softie and told me to stop crying before he'd say another word. Then he said he didn't know how to reach Bob in Squaw Valley, but that I should call his mother and he gave me her number.

I dialed and Marylee Futernick answered. I introduced myself and said I needed Bob's telephone number. She had no idea who I was but didn't seem surprised. She then said that Bob did not have a phone.

"But here's what you can do," she explained. "Tomorrow, call the postmistress at the Tahoe City Post Office. Say there's an emergency and you have to reach Bob Futernick. Ask her to put a note in his mailbox with your name and number on it. When he picks up his mail, maybe he'll call."

The next day I called the postmistress and asked her to put this note in Bob's mailbox: "A problem has come up and I need your help. Please call me." I gave her my name and phone number and she was accommodating.

Bob called me that evening. It was invigorating to hear his voice and we both felt surprised we had made this reconnection. I wanted to flirt and perhaps get a sense from Bob that he'd found me attractive, but I remembered my mission and did my best to relay the downbeat sequence of the past few days. I invited him to come to Berkeley on Friday so we could talk about my boyfriend. He was surprisingly nice about this foolish plan and said he would drive down. I made it clear there was a Murphy bed in the living room where he would sleep.

On Friday evening my heart bounded as I opened the door. Bob looked so appealing with his small green Travelaire suitcase (we still own it!) and ready smile. This time my hug was not so chaste.

I'd cooked linguini with marinara sauce for him and Wendie, whom I'd invited to join us. Over dinner she and I listened as Bob told about having broken his neck in a ski accident in Squaw Valley a year and a half before. He relayed the event without drama but it was shocking. Wendie and I felt so grateful that he had not only survived, but was ambulatory and appeared to be fine. We were, however, amazed he was still living in Squaw Valley and had a season lift ticket.

Bob also told stories about his brother Ken and the practical jokes they used to play on each other, and how he was trying to give his sister Laura, eleven, art lessons, and that his married sister Gail had just found out she was pregnant. Wendie shared stories about being one of five daughters, all born in Idaho, all living now in California. I told about my own travels—for me, on the East Coast—and noted that the fourteen-year-span of my siblings almost exactly matched Bob's, though Bob was the oldest and I was the third.

Conversation flowed as if we were old friends, but while Bob spoke I had to practically sit on my hands. I wanted to stroke his cheek, run my fingers through his thick hair, grab his hand and kiss him. Even on that late-October evening in 1969, the second night I had seen him, I could not get enough of his face.

After pasta, Sara Lee pound cake and Constant Comment tea— and the three of us hand-washing and toweling dry the dishes—Wendie left to spend the weekend with her boyfriend. I changed into my flannel Lanz nightgown and went to the bathroom to prepare for bed.

The amber-colored Neutrogena soap gave off a refreshing scent as I washed my face. At that moment I knew I wanted to become lovers with Bob. I went into the living room where I had prepared the Murphy bed with clean sheets.

"Where do you want me to sleep?" I asked. "In my bedroom or here?"

Soon the nightgown was off and we were savoring the nearness of each other's bodies and I, too, was sleeping in the Murphy bed.

The next day, before Bob and I drove to San Francisco to have brunch with my mother and sister, he asked me to choose a book that was special to me and to bring it with us. As we drove across the Bay Bridge—on this trip it was morning and the sun was behind us—I felt lucky that I might have an alternative to Steve.

The bagels and lox brunch at my mother's apartment gave me another chance to observe Bob. His banter with her was relaxed because they knew each other. And he showed genuine interest as Nancy spoke about her recent school experience, one so different from North Carolina, because in San Francisco she attended middle school in Chinatown and was the only Caucasian in her homeroom. Her best friends were Daisy and Pansy Louie. Sour plum candy, which these sisters ate every day after school, had become her favorite new snack.

It was clear that Nancy was enjoying sharing these details and she was delighted to learn that Bob was a serious Giants fan. Her enthusiasm was topped only by hearing that Bob's father had been a professional baseball player. In fact, had played shortstop with the San Francisco Seals, the Pacific Coast Team that preceded the Giants.

The four of us said an affectionate goodbye and Bob took me to his family's bindery on Bryant Street where he rebound, in teal leather and gold-leaf lettering, the book I had brought along: *The Family of Man*. One reason I loved that book from an exhibit at the Museum of Modern Art is that the first quotation that accompanies a photograph is the end of Molly Bloom's soliloquy from *Ulysses*...the gorgeously lyrical part about *yes*.

Bob and I were alone in the bindery. We kissed in that industrial space—and there was an extended kiss draped over a working table where he was taking apart the book. When I recovered my composure and could focus on the bookbinding, I noted how he prepared the skin of leather before gluing it to new cardboard covers, attached blue-and-green marbled endpapers to the inside of the covers, and heat-impressed, in gold, the title in the lower right-hand corner of the front cover. Then, with a heated tool resembling a pizza cutter, he embossed four straight lines emanating from the title, like four bright rays of the sun.

That evening we ate dinner at Edsel Ford Fong's restaurant in Chinatown and saw a Buster Keaton movie at the Surf Theatre. Being together felt easy and he made me laugh. Although it was not literally true, I felt I had not laughed in a long time. By Sunday night when Bob drove back to Squaw Valley, we knew we were falling in love.

There had been a girl he'd been dating, though, and manners told me I had to explain a version of these events to Steve. I called him the following night and, to my surprise and confusion, he was again interested in me.

The following weekend Bob drove down from Squaw Valley but

I saw Steve one night, Bob the next, and Steve the next. Rather than feeling flattered, I felt terrible. By the fourth night my indecision was making me sick. I called my mother and asked if I could come home.

As soon as I arrived at her apartment I explained my distress. She was genuinely sympathetic but for reasons I now admire declined to offer advice. I went into Nancy's bedroom where she was completing a ninth-grade math assignment. I told her about the ping-ponging of the previous week and what a mess my life felt like.

"Nancy, I really don't know what to do. Please, help me out here."

"Go with Bob," she answered without hesitating. I then remembered that first moment I had looked at Bob at the Abrams' house.

This December we will celebrate our fortieth anniversary.

A Provident Liquor Store

MEETING AT THE play *Hair* in 1969 might have predestined that Bob and I would have a hippie wedding. No engagement ring, no bridal shower, no bridesmaids or best man or limousine, no professional photographer and certainly no tropical honeymoon. We had a potluck reception at my mother and stepfather Jerry's house in Belmont after the ceremony, and spent our wedding night in my stepsister Sheryl's bedroom, which she'd gamely vacated.

Weddings can cost tens of thousands of dollars. Ours cost $200, including the wine glass.

I wrote our invitations by hand, paid $4.75 for my thread-thin gold wedding band, made my own tiny red rose bouquet, and asked my friend Rachel Goodman (Benny's daughter!) to sew my wedding dress from cranberry velvet bought on sale. The eyelet cotton sleeves and ruffle around the collar added only a few extra dollars. Though I already owned the white boots I wore, I did buy new white tights. It was mid-December but unseasonably warm so I didn't need a sweater or shawl.

Actually, I was pretty elegant compared to Bob. An hour before our 2 P.M. wedding in Rabbi Joseph Asher's study at Temple Emanu-El, Bob and I left Mom and Jerry's house where we'd been staying for several days and dashed by my brother Elliot's house in Daly City. Bob rummaged through Elliot's closet to find something to wear to our wedding.

In about ten seconds Bob emerged with a navy-blue blazer that more or less fit. He grabbed a dark tie as well, and the slacks he was already wearing were good enough. We got into our green Chevrolet pickup truck and sped to San Francisco. This slapdash sartorial success made us feel jolly about the rest of the afternoon. Wedding planning? Not really necessary.

But when we were on Geary Street, five blocks from the Temple, I realized I'd forgotten the wine glass, symbol of the destruction of the Babylonian Temple smashed at the end of a Jewish wedding. I'd left it wrapped in a white linen napkin on my mother's kitchen counter, thirty miles away. Tears welled. We may have crafted an alternative-style wedding but I wanted Bob to stomp on that wine glass. I wanted to hear the seventeen family members crowded in the rabbi's study cry out a joyous *Mazel Tov!* I had my reasons.

Bob's parents had divorced after their twenty-fifth wedding anniversary. Because he'd witnessed the pain of their dissolving relationship as well as revelations of his father's infidelity and his mother's desolation, he did not want to get married. He feared marriage would ruin our relationship.

It was 1971. The year before (during People's Park riots in Berkeley), gas tanks, tear gas, the National Guard, and a shooting had felt like military experiences. The atmosphere was dangerous and depressing. To my mother's dismay, I left U.C. Berkeley in June 1970, twenty-two units short of graduation to live with Bob in Grass Valley. (I did go back in spring of 1973 to graduate.)

Bob and I lived in a house deep in the woods. He found odd jobs as an electrician and handyman, and set up a bookbindery in the basement of the house where he worked on commissions from his father's bindery in San Francisco. I was a waitress in a Chinese restaurant. We did not need much money: rent for each of us was $35 a month.

I missed the intellectual stimulation of Berkeley and hated the thought of facing another rainy Grass Valley winter with heat from one fireplace and two wood-burning stoves. But I was unconflicted about living with Bob. Each month we were learning what it meant to be in a trusting relationship. We baked bread, grew vegetables, raised chickens. With several roommates, our house was sort of a commune, each of us trying to embody the best of the peace-and-love '60s.

Still, I was clear I wanted to get married. At twenty-two I had already weathered one failed love relationship, had an affair in Paris with an American named Gary, and endured a series of bad hookups in between. It may sound funny but I was feeling like an old maid, fearful I would not share my life with one man or become a mother, the only career goal I ever had. I lay awake at night wondering why I couldn't convince Bob to marry me: *Trust me, it will work out. Please, just do it for me. Can't you see that the institution of marriage is wonderful. I want this and I can't believe you don't.*

One night in mid-October I realized this arguing, this pleading, was indeed ruining our relationship. No matter how cogent my line of reasoning seemed to be, I sensed Bob would not change his mind. Before falling asleep I gave up hope that we would marry.

In the morning I opened my eyes, noticed it was raining, sat bolt upright, turned to Bob, and proposed. He said yes.

For the two months between deciding to marry and the actual December day, I would dream of the moment we'd be pronounced husband and wife—and hear that comforting sound of the glass smashing. The whole morning of December 17 I felt calm, almost chirpy, like a dressed-for-the ball Cinderella. As a child, that was my favorite movie. I adored hearing the birds tweet as they sewed her powder blue ball gown, using just their beaks to perform the handiwork and their cheer to make her beautiful. Now I was a wreck over a single glass. Then I spotted a liquor store on that very block of Geary Street.

"Bob, stop the car and give me some money!" I cried. "I'm going to run into this liquor store and buy a wine glass."

He checked every pocket, including the ones in Elliot's coat, and could find only a single dollar bill. I had not brought a purse. I spotted a quarter on the floorboard.

"Don't worry, I'll figure something out," I shouted as I pushed hard on our creaky pickup door and ran into the liquor store, holding my long dress up so it wouldn't drag on the sidewalk.

The store clerk was sitting behind the cash register, looking bored.

"Do you have any really cheap wine glasses?" I asked, trying not to screech. This middle-aged man seemed unfazed that a young woman with a cranberry velvet gown and waist-length hair all gussied up was asking for a single wine glass at 1:50 on a Friday afternoon.

"I do," he said and pointed to the limited glassware section of the store. I spotted a wine glass, ran to the shelf in relief and brought the glass to the counter.

"That'll be $1.25 plus tax," he said.

"Oh God," I thought.

"I have the $1.25 but no tax. Please...I'm getting married in ten minutes and I *really* need this wine glass."

"OK, honey, the tax is on the house. Have a great marriage," he said as I ran out of the liquor store and jumped back into the truck. Bob and I sped up the remaining five blocks and, mercifully, found a parking space.

By now it was seconds before two o'clock. Our respective families had gathered in Rabbi Asher's study. I had known him since I was eleven. He had been my rabbi at Temple Emanu-El in Greensboro, North Carolina, officiating at my confirmation when I was fourteen. He was now rabbi at Temple Emanu-El in San Francisco, officiating at my wedding when I was twenty-two.

I prayed he would have a white handkerchief we could borrow for wrapping around the wine glass. (It hadn't occurred to me that the Temple might have an extra wine glass!) He did, and we placed the wrapped glass in front of Bob's feet.

Bob and I held hands as the rabbi explained, in his German-inflected accent, that it was difficult for him to articulate how much this ceremony meant to him. He'd known me since I was in the seventh grade and we had been through many turbulent times together in Greensboro. We had each traveled with our families, he said, to this beautiful city. And he could definitely see how Bob and I would be good together. Then he uttered that magisterial sentence: "And now with the power vested in me by the state of California, I declare you husband and wife." Bob smashed the glass and the joyful cheer rang out. We earned that *Mazel Tov*.

End of an Argument

After torrents of words
calm falls
in a fine mist.

Cold breathing
warms
toes relax.

We fall in love
with words
each other
all over again.

Options grow wider
in parentheses of embrace
not possible
minutes before.

Flannel

When it's new it can be smooth as felt and just as thick.
Who could foretell the thrashings it would take in the washer,
endless turnings in the night. At first, wrapped in tissue,
it can't know the twists awaiting it, the sleepless hours
of retreat and surrender, the comfort it would be called to give
when color had been leached and cotton felt like bone.
Later, wearing thin and soft like gauze, skin almost showing
underneath, it's not much protection any more. It serves
a different purpose now: reminder to wrap the blankets around tightly,
to warm each other silently. Heat comes from the lasting of years.

Harmony Broke Out

A LONG MARRIAGE translates to many thousands of days and millions of moments. Who can give narrative to something so complex? How do you amply salute something that's ripe for dime-store sentiment? In the jumble of marital experiences are delicious moments, passages of despair and, sometimes, not much feeling at all. There are periods of transgression and periods of such closeness that you can feel like a combination of primary colors, the way yellow and blue become green.

Still, Valentine cards make it sound so easy, and marriage often *is* easy, but there are hundreds of reasons marriages falter. Mine has, numerous times.

For months in 1978, my husband was attracted to another woman. We lived through that painful spring, groping for what had brought us together in the first place. Patience, tears, and even a bit of black humor got us through. By summer it was as if our marriage had finally begun in earnest. A few years later I foolishly engaged in a flirtation. Just a few kisses and conversations that went beyond friendly, but these were hurtful to my husband and wracked me with guilt.

Then, it seemed, the real work began. We had, of course, had early moments of delight. We were happy we decided to marry and had chosen each other. But we were fighting, entering sticky arenas of control. Over the years, however, and countless hours of talking—often in the middle of the night with insomnia on our side—we learned to take our hurts more lightly and to listen less defensively. We made the choice to accept each other. Harmony broke out.

Now, sometimes I'll be loading the dishwasher or sitting next to Bob at one of our children's graduations, or he and I will be dancing and I'll look at this man and feel like a teenager in love. Only luckier. We survived the shoals of young love to luxuriate in mature love.

We never expected to be part of a minority: two people who married young, stayed married to each to other, reared our children, lived all of our marriage in the same city (and in just one apartment and then one home) and celebrated several milestone anniversaries.

Many experiences could have brought us to the brink: chronic pain that we have both experienced, back-to-back deaths of a parent and a sister, alcoholism in our family, bouts of depression, the harrowing night we thought our son had died in a streetcar accident (our son was fine), money problems, religious differences, and the countless challenges that parents, especially parents of adolescents and then twenty- or thirtysomethings, tumble into. The chaos of life shared.

Yet prevailing—continuing—is itself renewing. Now our deepest pleasure is the generosity we feel toward each other. The gratitude we share for getting through all those dark moments of the night. Increasingly Bob and I delight in each other's successes, and trumpet them unabashedly to anyone who will listen.

A friend once told me, in the bloom of new love, that it was as if she and her boyfriend wanted to proffer the best morsels on their plate to one another. At this later stage of our marriage, that sense of "What can I give you?" brings an even greater bounty.

There's comfort in that philanthropy. After years, we have found faith in each other. Accepted that troubles will arise because they always do—and occasionally a hurricane will blow in—but somehow peace in the house will prevail. That maybe, just maybe, we had fought all our serious arguments. That after all these years we'd located love that's mutual and truly unconditional.

Bed School

We sleep in an 1897 white oak carved bed
its provenance: Maine
traveling through so many states as it migrated west.
Now it has crossed a second century.
We purchased it in California,
that is where we sleep in it.

Our bed is a study hall,
conjugating verbs to weep, to worry, to want, to give.
By now nearly all verbs have occurred in this bed.

Tonight
we are students of literature
reading the same Israeli novel, two copies,
See Under: LOVE.

My heart quickens as I get out of bed for a glass of water—
you, with reading glasses, parsing those difficult words.
Separate and together we read, will be reading
one author's runnels of sorrow and death
and the sly eternal power of imagination.
Let me freeze this moment
this image distilling years together
as you study that perfectly titled book.
Let me return to this image
like a penciled note pulled out of my pocket
or an answer penned ahead of time on my hand
when after all these years, all these nights
I can still fail in remembering your love
though you reassure me, often.

You left a note one morning on the back of your business card,
placed it on the desk in the window near our bed
reminding me in fine black lines that you know me, love me.
I study that small card each time I walk past the window,
your words purposeful as a building's cornerstone.

Occasionally I will awake after you've gone
and notice editorials, articles
I've ripped out for you
scattered over the quilt or landed on the floor.
When I straighten the sheets and fluff our pillows
I am surprised you completed my assignment,
our double bed a place of learning.
I allow a smile, the kind I save
when I remember something
I taught you or you taught me about the night.

When One Weeps, the Other Tastes Salt

That's a one-line poem I read when I was fifteen.

Don't remember much poetry but that line is hard to forget:
a seven-word poem titled *Marriage*, as compressed as poetry itself.
At fifteen, I thought I understood those words
but decades of marriage reveal their truth.

Still, I like to give a new bride a saltcellar,
for a feel for salt is one hallmark of a fine cook
and a good wife.
Shared tears, too, though this is hard to say at a bridal shower.

Too much salt and the taste dominates,
shutting out other flavors
delicate herbs and spices in gravies or stews.
Too much and the dish is ruined,
it burns the tongue.

So is it with marriage.
Too caustic a way of talking
and bitter becomes dominant.
It's the harsh taste that lingers.

All relationships carry this possibility.

Forget the salt
and perfectly concocted mixtures have barely any taste,
any pop.
Salt marries flavors.
Even the sweetest dessert requires a pinch of salt.

Without salt—ardor, chemistry, empathy—
love doesn't linger, become more subtle
or notable to the palate.

Pepper adds pungency but is almost never sufficient.

With a life's partner
be generous with salt,
gentle in its delivery.
Just as a cook (or bride, or groom) learns to correct for seasoning
at the end of a recipe
or the start of a marriage
stop, play with roles of salt and cellar,
spice and medium, the funny and the lachrymal.
Adjust. Forgive. Repeat.
Together.
When moved, let yourself
taste the tears.

If You'd Be My Old Man, I'd Be Your Sea
words on the front of a blank card purchased at
The Booksmith on Haight Street

If you are the surprise of morning
I will wash in dawn's hope

If you are the cultivator of lilacs
I will bathe in that purple scent

If you are the sanctuary for sadness
I will bring you, in my skirt, all my sorrows

If you are the lamp of kindness
I will immerse in arcing light

—for Bob on his 65th birthday

Selecting Wallpaper

Les Sauvages de la Mer Pacifique, made in 1806 by Joseph Dufour,
is a series of woodblock-printed wallpapers from the Age of Enlightenment
offering knowledge-enhancing art about Pacific islands,
but no one in these scenes looks remotely Polynesian.
Figures resembling, instead, mythic Greek characters
tiptoeing in Napoleonic shoes, women wearing Empire-waisted gowns
and men sporting draped robes and Grecian helmets.

South Pacific composition of aqua trees against a clouded blue sky—
a Frenchman's view of island paradise (although Dufour never traveled
past Europe). More than 220 figures are pictured, including a small dog
with his snout in a wicker lunch basket, but in Panel Three
there is the jarring scene depicting the death of Captain Cook
by spears wielded by enraged Hawaiians.

This panorama of wallpapers is slightly silly
yet it is my favorite art at the de Young Museum,
my husband having repaired these vignettes as paper conservator in 1975,
ten strips of wallpaper rolled tight as player piano rolls, and he
relaxed them, reattached flecks of color, inpainted losses
and assessed their beauty.

Now they hang as ten smooth panels
and he, thirty-six years later, is Associate Director,
his office one floor below this gallery.

To me he is a conservator, still,
bringing a discerning eye, skilled hand,
understanding the hazards
that threaten any work of art,
the potential for damage in any created thing.

I want to touch these wallpapers
as if they are the years he and I have touched:
all the hurts and helps, assessments and gazes
he and I have cast upon the other,
a vision, even when one turned away
or the shutters came down.
I look at these wallpapers and see our marriage.

In 1975 we were newlyweds,
our early years earnest, buoyant, scarred.
Still, there was hope our marriage, that original creation
like these Dufour panels,
would not disintegrate
and skilled repairs
and assessing beauty would become habit.

It is 2011.
The abilities to see
that made Bob a skilled conservator
and that I have honed in my desire to observe
have transformed the way
we look at each other.

Wallpapers, side-by-side, touching the future.

Children

Bird and Nest

Disappearing the Night Frost

At eight, Jacob
you feel heavy on my lap
but your weight
grounds me like a divining rod.
With my face in your hair
I could drink you like a spring.

Boyish love restores me now.
Though I have sent you
crouching behind doors
hot tears jumping from your eyes
when you stand, I am quieted.
Like the sun
that disappears the night frost
your face stems my fury
transforms my rage into surprise
and you, standing there,
iridescent like a pearl,
bless me with your forgiveness.

Air Baseball

A man on the corner plays flute
and you, long legs
sporting new tennis shoes
nylon black shorts
fish from my wallet two
quarters for ice cream,
then flip them noiselessly
in the green velvet-lined case.
The guy calls "Hey!"
silver bat extended
over imaginary home plate
and you
throw one perfect pitch
to the air of his flute.

Carful of Boy, 1994

I DIDN'T GO to the prom in high school, though I would have loved to have been invited. The few school dances I did attend in the mid-1960s were endless evenings of waiting to dance. Those were the years before girls asked boys to dance or asked them out on dates, or nobody dated at all.

And I stayed in the freshman dorm most Saturday nights, listening to Joni Mitchell or Judy Collins or the Jefferson Airplane with the two or three other dateless girls on the third floor. Some weekend nights we would put on make-up to imagine ourselves desirable as we studied American history texts, or I would color just my lips in consolation for the sadness of geology. All those tectonic shifts and centuries of rock filled me with a vague sense of defeat as I read my class notes. The fact that the "mountains were uplifting" did not comfort me. I felt as lonely as those rocks.

In my heart I knew I would make a great date, with lots of facts to share and affection to give and even a few jokes to tell, but mostly I remained a latent date during those formative years. Boys did not see me, at least that's what I believed. I felt invisible in the presence of cuter, flirtier girls and wished they would vanish so boys would see *me*. Surprisingly, these wallflower images remain, years later, no matter what affairs of the heart I have enjoyed or how appealing I may feel as a woman.

But now I have a son, age fifteen, and as I drive him and three of his junior varsity teammates to a Saturday baseball game, I have four boys in my car and I imagine all of them as dates I might have had in high school or even those early years of college. They are mine, I smile to myself.

The four of them fill my car with their rangy boyness, their varying tallness, one already shaving, though at 10 A.M. on Saturday morning he is so clean-shaven my finger wants to touch his cheek. All of them have a similar haircut: long on the top, short on the sides but with their maroon baseball caps on it is difficult to tell.

Around the edges of their white uniforms with maroon letters and numbers, I notice biceps forming, the hair on their arms thickening, their feet probably still growing. As they recount each hit and error of their last baseball game, their voices wobbling around the lower registers and full-face laughter punctuating each play, they often talk at once. They joke about their obsession with baseball cards when they were younger, debate who will be next year's pitcher, and agree that so-and-so is really a lame player. Variations on the baseball theme are endless and girl talk is absent. After all, they're suited up and on their way to play ball!

As they talk, unaware of my listening, I breathe in their slightly musky scent mixed with dust from their cleats and the fresh smell of laundry detergent and I wonder, Did *their* mothers go to the prom? Do those mothers feel this delighted to have four high school boys in the car? Do they wish they could be traveling forever? Out of nowhere, the tallest boy thanks me for giving him a ride as we breeze over the Bay Bridge to warmer weather and I am surprised how quickly my eyes fill. They are mine, at least for this car ride, and they cannot possibly know my happiness.

This carful of boy is late payment with interest for all those boyless afternoons of July and August, yearning for the scent of honeysuckle to mix with the feel of a boy's hand ruffling the hairs of my arm. Or when I dreamed I was riding in a boyfriend's car as he held one hand on the steering wheel while the other capped the shoulder of my blouse and we sat next to each other and listened to music on the radio. In this dream I would be silent; it would be enough just to sit next to him, driving on a Saturday afternoon and wishing this ride would never end.

Decades later I have a husband and a daughter, but it is my son who is the antidote to all those years of feeling invisible. Every day now I revel in the proximity of boys—my son's friends, his teammates, his classmates, himself—and the chance to rub away that old feeling of being overlooked.

The strange thing is that I need nothing from these boys to feel almost giddy in their presence. I love when they talk to me and of course I love when my teenage son talks to me, but their nearness is enough.

Today in my car, as I am surrounded by this boy energy, I revel in the mysteries that confounded me when I was younger but charm me now as a mother. Charm me even as my son and his friends begin their own cycle of mystifying girls—though they will do it, I believe, more sweetly and perhaps with a sense of apology.

As I pull into the parking lot of the East Bay high school, I realize: If only I'd known how to bask in the difference of boys when I was younger, delighted in the species of *boy* rather than foundered with it.

As the doors open, my son and his friends pile out of the car and we all walk to the baseball diamond. Once again I smile to myself. I have a son who eases that boy sorrow I never thought I'd shake.

My Son's Heartbeat

In early November the first sound was your heartbeat
tiny but *there*
medical stereo broadcasting from the stethoscope on my abdomen
your first rhythm-and-blues sound—
doo-wop doo-wop whoosh-whoosh
the beat of my heart lurching with yours.

I know nothing of making hearts—
aorta, auricles, ventricles, vena cava, the four chambers—
no knowledge of blood gasses or platelets
or the crafting of internal organs.
Yet here it was: a perfect heart forming.

In mid-April the first sound was the midwife's authoritative
"the cord, the cord" wrapped round your neck three times.
No lusty wail, first sound of life.
Your long skinny body
waxy and grey,
your head wet with black hair—
you looked so somber, a baby patriarch,
my Jacob.

The doctors took you to an isolette in the room,
blew oxygen past your face from a clear plastic tube
and you pinked up,
your yowl soft but increasingly *there*.

Around midnight the first night you came home
nestled in my bed,
torso barely bigger than my hand—
your chest
up and down, up and down, even in sleep,
proving lungs, heart, blood—
and I asked myself
"How do you know to do that?"

Late August, nearly thirty years later
you and I are dancing
a slow dance at your cousin's wedding.
You are so tall my head comes just to your heart
as I lay it against the stripes of your brown and white shirt
just to the right of the tie you borrowed from Dad.
My ear resting on your thin chest
I listen to the insistent swish

the *doo-wop doo-wop whoosh-whoosh*
pump like the soft drum of the band.
I don't want this song to end
and though we dance among many
it is only your heart
I hear.

My Daughter and Water

I saw my obstetrician last night; twenty-six years later
he still emphasizes the water—her *water birth* but that's not correct.
She was born in the bathroom, not in the water.

I labored in the Alternative Birth Center, hospital home
of low-tech births, music tapes and regular beds. I even took a shower,
washed my hair, refreshed and helped by the stream of hot water.

But I labored too slowly. Only centimeters dilated after seven hours,
the membrane still intact. The doctor took an instrument that resembled
a crochet hook, ruptured the sac of amniotic water.

Nature's pouch attached to the womb, bag where the baby grows and
cavorts, but birth distress can cause meconium, earliest stools
of the baby, to be released in the water.

Suddenly: stunning contractions and we had to take the elevator
to the labor room. Then almost everyone left to change into
scrubbing greens. Agonizing, I occasionally sipped ice water.

For a few minutes I clung, low, like a lead ball in a slingshot, to my friend
Sara, the only person now with me. "Take me to the bathroom," I begged.
Splitting with pain, I could think only of the comfort near water.

I grunted like an animal above the toilet as the baby slid into the birth canal,
crowned: her web of matted dark hair. Bob, changed into scrubbing greens
and back with me, felt her head, held me to stand away from the water.

He ran to get the doctor who was calling the pediatrician for help.
Standing fully up I screamed and watched the baby slide out.
Sara caught her; she had just washed her hands with soap and water.

Then my brother Elliot, a doctor, rushed in, said, "She's a good baby"
—a medical term and her uncle was correct! Not blue from aspirating
meconium. Lungs clean like flowing spring water.

I took the receiving blanket from his hands as he rushed to get help.
Sara and I holding my baby Sarah opened the door to a sea
of surprised people. Walked out as if parting the water.

Full medical staff: *Code Blue* had been called. Still, no scissors
could be found to cut the umbilical cord, no basin
for the vernix-cleansing bath of clear water.

At last the baby and I were in a hospital bed after nurses cleaned her.
I held this female body with a familiarity I had never known before.
She sucked knowingly, like a fierce and beautiful fish taking to water.

Night Child

I wanted you so badly
sometimes I think I stole you from the night.
No wonder you have a chilling beauty.

You came into life
a high diver reversing the plunge—
jumped glistening from the water and splashed into the air

acting as your own midwife.
Now at four you ask fact-of-life questions
Why are mothers a little bit sad? Why do ladies cry?

I have no answers for you, Sarah
but think when your namesake laughed
to hear she would bear Isaac at ninety
she must have known a child
could warm the shivery darkness.

Lace

"Five planets in Scorpio," an astrologer exclaimed
the week you were born
the astrological chart she drew for you so lopsided
all the lines were scrunched in the left-hand corner of the chart.
When you were quite young
I could discern those crabbish tendencies.

More often
I would think of that astrological chart
and think it…wrong,
the sweetness of your nature matched by your depth, unexpected
for one so young, questions and metaphors
any poet would envy—
some of your words at two, three, and four:
   allness at death
   thirst of babies who never cry
   heartbreak of labor
   time of a hundred o'clock.

You are as if I closed my eyes
and willed you transported from my own girlhood, only happier
wiser, calmer, with even-spaced teeth and curly hair
your beauty as intricate
as the designs your great-grandmother Anna Leah tatted.
Your Hebrew name: Sarah Leah.

I look at your small body as if edges, ineffable frills
evaporate, then reform
the way a tatter assesses, re-pins, reworks and approves
the pattern of her smart, intricate lace.

Retrieving Children's Blocks at 6 A.M.

Walking down the hall to take an early morning bath, I see
through sheer white curtains the red, green, yellow, and blue
of plastic blocks on my roof, surprise remains of
a child's high toss.

Startled by colors nosing through curtains, I slip
out the window, put my feet on particle-paper roofing
and fetch those blocks.

Then blocks in hand, I pause to feel the dawn, to smell
the cold damp sweetness in my nose,
to notice silver light, diaphanous, against the brown-black roof

to wear the chill as clothing on my skin, and stop
like a resting weather vane—

only to have my reverie broken by the frightened cry at 6 A.M.
of a neighbor's daughter waking to find a naked woman on the roof,
looking skyward.

Bird and Nest

Western Foundation of Vertebrate Zoology,
Camarillo, California, "Egg and Nest" exhibit

On a slightly browned field-note card typed in 1948
a detail about the California Brown Pelican—*Pelecanus occidentalis*—
"Voice: Adults silent (rarely a low croak). Nestlings squeal."

Young ones hunger; parents forage and feed.
Before I became a mother, my friend told me
when she has raspberries on her plate
she gives them to her young son.
She used to devour all raspberries.

What an infinity of nests:
sturdy twigs or fluffy parts of flowers,
whorled pine needles and gyroscopes of grapevines.
Even pearlescent strips of store-bought Easter-egg feathering
have been woven into nests, the real from the fake.

An oologist is an ornithologist who studies eggs.
So onomatopoetic: double *o*
exuberance from the mouth of the parent
when life emerges
and the open-mouthed squeal of the tiny one,
hungering throat of the newly hatched,
o as in the ovoid shape itself
physics of no sharp edges.

Does a brooding bird ponder the horizon
with regret for ways she will fail to nourish?

The cold night air braces and invigorates.
Her surging breast heats the nest.

Body

Decrements of Pain

Private Parts

In a poem, you show
your private parts
as matter-of-factly
as legs in the stirrups

Revealing folds and fissures
passageways to secrets
probings to the heart

Like dye, the ink articulates
the blemished cells on paper
as surely as any doctor's slide

The pen, a curette
scrapes scars and knots,
wounds
disclosing female troubles,
recurrent sorrows
at times unearthing healthy tissue

A poem is a speculum   opening
yourself, declaring
pleasure and pain,
a peepshow to parts normally veiled

In a poem, you say
with composure
words
that would silence a meeting
or startle a truce

But
what it reveals
brings nakedness,
not shame.

Spine

for Jon Lehrman, M.D.

Humans walk erect now, our spine—
that very word for courage—
a tower enumerating our back into vertebrae, discs, muscles
and one long yellow ligament,
ligamentum flavum. Yes, everyone has a long yellow streak
down his or her back
though at times
just standing up can be a feat of courage.

There's physics: Facets misaligned and inflamed—
wear and tear on discs causes them to flatten.
The fluid in the disc bulges on nerves
creating agony.

Memory, too: Must be—
so many people suffer back pain.
Those nether regions from childhood
stashed thoughts
lingering in the lumbar
pushing and tightening
screaming straight to the brain
all those hurts
trapped way back.

In time, fluid returns to the disc
a container reformed, re-hydrated,
furious pressed-on nerves relieved.

Walking helps,
walking tall helps,
limber looping stitch of a fluid spine
supple posture,
balm back in our backs.

Turning upside down helps,
anti-gravity
aligning discs like an old-fashioned coin changer
used by the Good Humor Man:
quarters where they're supposed to be,
then dimes, then nickels.

Memories can be upended, too:
looking them over, then placing them away
like storing old linens in a hope chest,
chastened with a strong wash of forgiveness
and the courage to acknowledge
past pains.

Decrements of Pain

Chronic pain is a plumb line
defining
dark regions, a root
always there
insistent
on attention
yet invisible
to others.

Emitting no
sound waves
within the body
it is a lowing
white noise
deafening
to the sufferer
silent to the observer.

Or it's a watch
with both arms splayed
flaccid from overwork
from unremitting ticking, tending
tedium—then, sometimes
with its own sense
of time and mystery
and all that medicine
can offer
the arms straighten
zero in on midnight
the hands of the clock
meeting like hands in prayer
this release
this analgesic
turning midnight
to noon
a decrease—
the medical term
decrements of pain
(opposite of increments)
please: *decrements* of pain
the three
most beautiful words
I have ever heard
in a doctor's office,
diminishment
loosening
of the thread
of hurt
and with patience, sometimes
a blessed
nothingness.

Get Well Soon
for Bobby Patri

Said so often and loosely
cavalier air
like *have a nice day, cheers, take care.*

The words on this card
get—well—soon
for you, recovering from surgery,
for me
can
feel fresh
the way a city feels after a long rain,
a long cry.

Three softly percussive syllables
jazzy word painting
brief aria to sing, or be sung
crooned like the night-sky's lullaby
cajoling whisper, gentle prod
to the weak and infirm
to jumpstart limbs, heart, will.

After surgeries, injuries, depression and pain,
death of my nephew Joshua
three days before his nineteenth birthday,
rending of the family,
I too have sought those words.

Get   well   soon.
Verb *Get*
as in gain, find once again.
Adverb *well* shows how to get or
in what direction to heal
as if it were simple, or linear.
Benedictive *soon*, long oo
slightly sad bleat of a foghorn
or cool radiance of a silver moon
cupped by two consonants.
When is soon?

It's the wishing and seeking
a deep, sweetwater, healing
replenishing well:
implied subject (*You*).

Surgery/Insomnia

Even as the anesthesiologist descends
the plastic mask over my face
preparing me to breathe deep

my mind shouts *insomnia*—
I will not be able to sleep.

I will feel the knife slice my betadined flesh
as the surgeon wields a diamond-cutter's precision.
Despite the ether I will feel my flesh
gush blood as it yields to the scalpel.

White pain will resist the stop
of anesthesia.

I will move from the surgical table
to the recovery room, mended by the surgeon
but shattered by the ordeal.

* * *

When I awake in the recovery room
the nurse hovering by my side
swaddles me in receiving blankets. I think
she is an angel. I have fast forwarded
through time, through some small sweet death
straight onto this soft white heaven.

The Day of Your Mastectomy
for Penny Lehrman

You ask your husband for carrot sticks.

In my dream you sit on a lawn-colored couch, quilt around your shoulders.
Behind you, a puffy flannel heart sewn as if by a child
is suspended by spindly wire.
On the table are narcissus, bulbous and fat
in the azure bowl, stalking up from stones.
Your husband hands you the carrot sticks.
He serves the stubby columns bunched in a clear glass,
like finger flowers.

Forget carrot sticks, I say from a corner of this dream.
Your mother died of cancer and you need fat.
Give up the ballerina's body sculpted from all those years.

Eat everything. French fries glistening in ketchup,
plump slices of blueberry pie, vanilla ice cream
warming down the sides into swirls as drops form on the plate.
And jelly doughnuts, not as good and warm as the ones
your mother brought home after her night shift
but still good.

Are carrots penance? Do I envy your famished beauty?
Who can figure out this dream.
It's awe you need, poems and prayers, talk and sweet consolation.

Insulate those erect shoulders, tall legs, calloused dancer's feet.
Sheathe your skull in softness before it sheds hair.
Pillow ribs, unsynchronous with stitches.
Cushion   oh cushion the heart.

Perfect Boy

for Ethan James Kee
(February 28, 1995–March 2, 1995)

Seven pounds, full term
then the unthinkable—

placental abruption
hemorrhage, rush to the hospital.

For those hours of life, three waning days,
each breath
still filled Lynn and Jeff with hopeful possibility.

Now, your parents and those who love them
hold your life in our lungs.

We say your name. Even silently
we retain its palpating sound,
relinquishment of your body—*Ethan*

heartbeat, always beating in the house of your parents,
two-syllable song of a name

each syllable percussing your parents' grief,
even as it will lift them
by the billionth breath
they will take from your death

the solidity of your name
constant as a pulse.

Blood in the Water

"Planet of the Jellies" exhibit
Monterey Bay Aquarium

In the tank
the jellyfish are
upside-down cups with flapping tendrils
scarlet arraying,
gossamer ribbon
the slenderest red in the water
How endometrial!
Tissue thinning
menstrual flow in a bowl
grief infusing the water,
the body's cry lasting for days.

Dress Rehearsal

The easy pain of this death

as I sit at the funeral
of a business acquaintance
or memorial service of a friend with whom I've lost touch
even an in-law
makes me shudder, anticipating the time

when no shared tears, loving eulogy
consoling cards

no orchid delivered
or casserole at the door
powerful embrace

will cool the loss
calm the shiver of grief
losing someone as close as oxygen,
this sameness, difference, kinship
that refracts image and sight
syncopates with breath
I call my own.

Faith

Imaginary Seder

The Gold Filling

My tongue runs over this newcomer, fluid and sinuous
as a sculpture of a swan. Only it is warm
and familiar and there
whenever I want it,
smoothest surface
I have ever known in my mouth.

There are other revelations.
One night I take a business book off the shelf—
no particular reason—
and turn to the acknowledgments, those spare warm words
a bonus to a librarian.
I read a tribute to Jeffrey Krames
the name I would have been given
if I had been a boy.

The next morning I make many calls,
find Jeffrey in New York.
He mentions his father,
where his grandfather was born in Poland
but tells me everyone else on this father's side was killed.
Certain he has no other relatives, he wants to get off the phone.
He has publishing work to do.

Perhaps he is right
but I tell him both our grandfathers are from Pechenezhyn,
Poland, now the Ukraine and before that Austria-Hungary.
(Does this explain his confusion, or mine?)
I say we spell our family names the same way.
I think my Aunt Sara once mentioned your father.
I would have been given your name.

Gathered around the kitchen table, over cups
of Maxwell House and slices of marble cake
aunts and uncles and parents spoke of food or children
occasionally of money or work,
never of lost relatives.

Now my tongue runs over this gold tooth
and I think of great-aunts and uncles
whose teeth were stolen, the gold removed.
What were their names?
Fania or Malka, Frederic or Otto?
Was their surname a single syllable like mine used to be,
Krames, or flourished with a Slavic ending?

Now I say Kaddish for these unnamed too,
this mourner's prayer always with me now
widening covenant burnished on Sabbath
metered syllables of palate and tongue and teeth

and thoughts still roam to Jeffrey Krames
not wishing to know me
yet named as if my twin.

Imaginary Seder

I'm the only full Jew I know of in Spoleto
Umbrian town of stone churches,
frescoes of Mary and angels rising.
Crossover country where paper-thin wafers and cups of crushed grape
are Christ's body.

This first night of Passover, accompanying my half-Jewish husband
with no extended family, no Seder
I will cross over, too.
At Ristorante Mercato in the town square
my husband and art colleagues and I order dinner.
I pass the bread basket as it comes my way,
breadsticks long and attenuated.

No leavened bread these eight days,
especially not this first Seder night
remembering dough prepared with no time to rise.
Bread of affliction from the days of Exodus.

I steer clear of croutons in my bowl of zuppa di funghi
but soon my spoon cannot avoid
these bursting vessels of leavening.
Forgive me, I say to no one.

No grape jelly taste of Manischewitz
but two bottles of dark Sagrantina.
Normally I sip one glass of dinner wine,
tonight I drink two full glasses
still falling short of the Passover four.

Shank bone, symbol of the lamb whose blood painted
the doorposts of Jewish houses
repelling the mythical angel of death.
I notice a lamb bone left on a plate at the next table.
I glance at it and think: looking will do.

Our table's bottle of aqua minerale will be *salt water*,
aftertaste of salty salad stand-in for Israelite tears.
No *roasted egg*, symbol of life itself,
so the egg pasta acts as understudy.

Light sprinkling of parsley—
not a whole sprig but still *karpas*,
intimation of spring and renewal.

Crushed hot pepper on the Spoletino pasta
transmutes to *horseradish*,
bitter symbol of slavery.

Charoseth—apples, nuts, cinnamon—
mortar of our ancestors used in Pharaoh's labor.
For dessert I order a baked pear,
the chocolate sauce sweeter than the charoseth
my family will eat tonight at their Seder in San Francisco.
Full and relaxed, we leave the restaurant
and walk into the cool night.

Stopping by the forno,
Spoleto's five-hundred-year-old bakery,
we watch bread being made.
Five bunches of beech wood, plumey and tall,
stand against the wall
like hoodlums congregating for a smoke.
Tonight they will burn
red hot in this ancient oven.

The solitary baker motions us inside,
air yeasty from hundreds of years of rising dough.
With floured hands, the baker stretches tomorrow's baguettes,
places each in a wooden trough worn smooth by years.
The loaves are separated by grey flannel runners
like priests' vestments.
The baker slashes hatch marks into the dough—
all those paintings of Christ,
tender area under Christ's nipple
pierced by the Roman spear.
Flick of the wrist of a baker
gives second meaning to bread of affliction.

The radio playing Italian opera:
Dayenu! It would have been enough!
Long song of slavery and redemption
so buoyant to me as a child at the Passover table
asking the question
"Why is this night different from all other nights?"
The baker transposed.
My father passing the plate of *matzos* stacked high,
beckoning to be broken.

Photosynthesis

...the solemn poetry, known only to chemists, of chlorophyll photosynthesis...

—*Primo Levi,* The Periodic Table

I. Newburgh, New York

I LEAVE BALMVILLE Elementary School on Wednesdays, released early from Mrs. Trombino's third grade: simple fractions, spelling, the dawning of science. A weekly yellow taxi shows up for me in the school parking lot. The cab driver takes me to Sons of Israel synagogue to study Hebrew in Mr. Davidowitz's class. In winter the sun is so hidden the afternoon sky is a cloudy stern grey. No buds yet, only latent growth sleeping deep within branches. December, January, and February are months so cold I wear padded woolen leggings under my dress when I board the school bus in the morning. Now these leggings cushion the back seat of the taxi.

For one year my parents, barely observant, belong to an Orthodox synagogue in Newburgh, sixty miles north of New York City. My grandfather who lives in Brooklyn is Orthodox, and when he visits, he attends this shul daily. His name is Louis; *Loeb* in Yiddish; *Lev* in Hebrew. I love the sound of that initialing L. L—last letter of the last word of the Torah: Is-ra-el.

I ace Hebrew spelling tests taken in the handwritten form of this ancient language that even as an eight-year-old in Mr Davidowitz's class I cannot hear enough of. Guttural *ch*, conjoined *tz*, whispery *sh*, helpful *aleph*—a—sometimes spoken, sometimes silent, its name almost an alphabet. In these weekly tests I love the feeling of the pencil keeping my right hand upright as the south side of my palm glides across lined paper, right-to-left, writing curlycued script of Hebrew. Some of the letters, *bet* and *vet*, b and v, look like tiny beaky birds preening in the sun. *Lamed*—l—a balanced crane standing on a looped leg. *Nun sofit*—n at

the end of the sentence—a vertical line, laddering. My favorite: *pay*—
p—tiny inward-spinning galaxy, perhaps the sun unspooling.

One time before class I ask Mr. Davidowitz if his wife is pregnant.
I had never asked anyone this question, but heard the rumor from my
mother. Mr. Davidowitz, who has three young children, smiles slightly,
says it is too soon to tell, that they will have to wait to see if things get
heavier. I do not understand his answer, or very much about the way life
germinates, but take it for a yes.

II. San Francisco, California

Sunday morning Hebrew class, Temple Emanu-El, five decades later,
I barely remember how to read the almost-on-fire printed Hebrew.
Those capital letters found in the Torah, prayer books, on gravestones.
But when pronounced by a rabbi or cantor, these are letters I thrill to.
My friend Gayle, new to Hebrew, and I, archaeologist of letters, spend
three years in a class studying with an Israeli woman in her seventies.
Her husband is dying of Alzheimer's. These mornings are her release
as she teaches prayer, especially Kaddish, mourner's prayer recited to
honor the dead but extolling God, and V'Ahavta, testament on loving
God but equally a reminder to be a person who loves.

Today is Gayle's sixty-fifth birthday. The Hebrew teacher and I and
twenty other women gather at Gayle's home for tea. I look at her, radi-
ant, and think: first all those fiery Hebrew letters and now you, a force
of light.

Biology spreads through the rooms. In her living room, walls painted sunshine, we drink tea and eat slightly salty sandwiches, then me-
ander to the family room, walls painted chlorophyll. Soft spring rain
outside. Air from sweet exhalations as her gratitude meets ours. Water,
CO_2, carbohydrates, salts, and sunlight. Photosynthesis: another subject I studied in the third grade. Even then photosynthesis seemed like
the world's poetry.

This party offers nourishment almost cellular. My friend the cata-
lyst as we gather and she circles the room explaining how she met each
one of us, her admiration, the qualities we emanate. On her birthday
she gives, and we brighten.

What Was, Was, and Is No More
Vos Geven Iz Geven Un Nito

I.

I CALL SARA to ask how she's handling these losses. Her mother died four weeks ago. The divorce from her second husband will be final soon. Tomorrow morning the movers will vacate the house she and Michael shared for eighteen years. The movers will leave. The new owner will come with the termite inspector.

As friends, Sara and I are intricately woven. She was my birth teacher when I was pregnant with Jacob; she helped deliver my daughter Sarah. In the backyard of her San Francisco home we recited Kaddish for Jerry Garcia, the rock musician who was Sara's long-divorced first husband. When she converted to Judaism, I was one of three women who accompanied her to the mikvah, the ritual pre-conversion bath.

Partly because I love Sara and partly because I love *things*, I want to help my friend sort through the gargantuan amount of stuff to be organized or disposed of before Sunday's garage sale. She'll need an extra pair of hands. This is not the ordinary detritus from eighteen years of living in one house.

There are at least two thousand dishes to sort through and wash and stack, plus scores of clocks, toasters, and watches. Piles of planters, candlesticks, vases, lamps, tureens, cameras, blankets, clothing, and typewriters. Michael, her second husband of thirty years, was a collector run amok.

Though a doctor by profession and a busy one, he thrift-stored or flea-marketed every week, then stashed his finds in every possible corner of the house, garage, backyard shed or basement.

Michael had already moved out. On Sunday Sara would attempt to sell all the *stuff* in a few hours, the only benefit being that she would get whatever money the sale brought in. That meant selling dishware ranging from the valuable to the bargain-basement—Bauer, McCoy, Fiestaware, Lu-Ray Pastels, Laurel of California Speckleware, Heathware, and Melmac—plus lots of mid-century modern collectibles and plenty of junk.

Over the years Michael's acquisitiveness would drive Sara to distraction. Now Sara, the ascetic, wants little of this stuff except for a few pieces of furniture and family history to keep for her children—Heather, her daughter with Jerry, and her two children with Michael: Julian and Molly. She does, however, want to keep the Heathware.

When she married for the first time in 1963, brown Heathware with eggshell enamel interior was the only thing she registered for. Her marriage to Jerry Garcia ended three years later, but Sara kept the brown and eggshell dishes. For many years Michael bought Sara any style of Heathware he could find. Greens, browns, rare black, and even the brown with eggshell interior when it showed up. On this cleaning-up day there were hundreds of pieces of Heathware spread out on the floor, as if waiting to be tagged from a dig.

Early the next morning I carry a basket with a thermos of Irish Breakfast tea, plus crumpets and jam, to Sara's house just two blocks up the hill. I include a small turquoise vase in the shape of a baby bootie, bought on a whim at a thrift shop. I fill the bootie with flowers from bushes Sara and I transplanted from her house to mine two years ago.

I arrive at the same time as the movers, three Israeli guys who work at the speed of light. At $80.00 an hour the movers get Sara's attention.

While she's with the movers I remove cobwebs and dirt from the dishes. Having my hands submerged in warm sudsy water feels soothing. The Heathware is beginning to shine, as are stacks of other dishes, including a huge assortment of speckled Laurel of California. I towel dry and re-sort mountains of plates, cups, saucers, and serving dishes in preparation for Sunday's sale.

Sara and I have only ten minutes to eat before she dashes off to meet the movers at her rental storage space. Because the movers have taken all the chairs, we sit in the middle of the living room on a rolled carpet. The breakfast tea is still hot, and delicious with milk and sugar. By now the toasted crumpets are cold. We imagine the apricot jam as salve for an emptying house.

"Boulevard of Broken Dreams," a song my mother used to sing to me in a deep warbly voice, runs through my mind. I tell this to Sara who looks at me and says, "What promise this house held!"

We hold each other and cry. She's mourning just about everything. I'm saying goodbye to a house I have come to love, and to Sara's neighbor nearness. I remember her "Synchronous Forty-four" birthday party in the large living room, her son Julian's Bar Mitzvah reception in the backyard. I remind Sara of these happy times.

Unlike any of my other friends, Sara and I often sing to each other. Perhaps that's because she used to perform Old-Timey music with Jerry Garcia in the pre-psychedelic '60s, and continues to enjoy singing. I like to express myself in lyrics, especially to her.

Finishing our makeshift breakfast, I sing Sara something I'd recently heard at a Yiddish music concert, another song my mother used to sing to me. *Vos Geven Iz Geven Un Nito*—What was, was, and is no more. As full of succor as this morning has been, Sara and I know something very big is over. But we will rototill this experience, too, into the loamy thing that is our friendship.

I'm late for work and Sara needs to meet those movers, but before we leave I give her the bootie vase with flowers. What should we call this offering?

A house-cooling present, we decide.

II.

At the garage sale the following Sunday, Sara is too anxious to deal with money or the hordes of bargainers so her friend Annette and I handle transactions. We sell what was probably one of the earliest Kodak cameras for $5.00. A pair of gold-plated antique glasses goes for a buck. Coveted Fiestaware plates and McCoy planters are exchanged for only a few dollars, though they'll be resold by dealers, no doubt, for much more.

During a break in the sale, Annette and I agonize over a hand-crocheted afghan. Should we sell it? What the heck, yes, we say, but it doesn't even get an offer. A Tibetan brass gong gets an offer of twenty-five cents. Sara, watching from the sidelines, steps in and says no, trying not to sound affronted.

A late-'50s foldable desk lamp, made of early plastic and chrome, something you might see in a design museum, gets an offer of $3.00. I can't let this piece of Americana go for a few dollars, especially since I know Sara bought it years ago as a gift for Jerry. I set the lamp aside to give to my son Jacob to take to college.

As the sale winds down, Sara, Annette, and I feel increasingly distressed by an antiques dealer who is driving a hard bargain for hundreds of pieces of that Laurel of California Speckleware. I want to shout at her, "Don't you realize today is about a shattering of a family? It's wrong of you to quibble over an already ridiculously low price for these dishes!"

I say nothing and leave a half hour before the garage sale is over.

III.

A month later, by chance, I walk into the antiques store owned by the woman who got all those Laurel of California for a song. When I see her I'm still annoyed, though I'd heard from Sara that the woman's demeanor changed once she learned that a thirty-year marriage was ending and a family was splitting up.

The owner recognizes me and her expression softens. "You know," she says, "I go to garage sales every weekend, and most have no emotional charge at all. But after your friend's, I just had to go home, sit on the bed with my dog, and think about what had happened. I still can't get it out of my mind."

I can't either, I tell her. Once again a fragment runs through my head, this time from *The Tempest*: "...such stuff as dreams are made on." She and I are, after all, in a shop loaded with other people's stuff. In one corner of the shop are stacks and stacks of speckled dishes waiting to be sold.

Saying Farewell to Joshua

*On May 13, 2003, around 4 P.M., I received a call from Ithaca,
New York. My brother-in-law Natan Huffman, my sister's husband, told me that Josh (their only son) had been a front-seat
passenger in an automobile accident. When Natan regained his
composure he said, in barely a whisper, that he didn't think Josh
was going to make it. I was the first family member he called.
Joshua died three hours later. Three days later, on what would
have been his nineteenth birthday, I delivered the eulogy for
Joshua George Huffman at a memorial service in Ithaca.*

TUESDAY AFTERNOON, just hours before I got the catastrophic
phone call from Natan, I had handwritten a letter to Andrew Solomon,
author of *The Noonday Demon: An Atlas of Depression*. I'd met Andrew
two years ago when he gave a reading at Temple Emanu-El in San Francisco, and had kept his card in my wallet for two years, never writing
to him. So the connection between posting that letter and a few hours
later finding myself crying and gasping for air on the phone with Natan
seemed...eerie.

Because, almost inexplicably, during the red-eye flight that I took
that night to Ithaca, I could not stop thinking of the first line of Solomon's nearly six-hundred-page book: *Depression is the flaw of love*. With
the specter of soon seeing my sister Nancy's face contorted with grief,
and Natan's as well, I thought: *No, loss is the flaw in love*. Because hovering over every love, especially our love for our children, is a loss that
none of us can bear. Yet it can be the very knowledge that our loved
ones could die, and die entirely unexpectedly, that makes us cherish
their nearness, their laughter, their touch.

But let's scramble those word tiles again and come up with this
sentence: *Love is the flow in life*. I've been whispering that mantra to
myself when I've been unable to sleep these past terribly difficult three
days. Love *is* the flow in life, and sometimes those we love most are
cruelly and prematurely taken from us, as Joshua has been.

Somewhere in that great, mysterious flow, embodied in every person in every seat in this room, is where I'll hold the spirit of my sweet nephew, youngest in Nana's lineup of five beautiful grandsons.

Josh, you would have been nineteen today. You were part boy who still slept every night with his "Ni-Ni," blue-green baby blanket now nearly rubbed smooth of color, and occasionally cuddled with Maynard, that goofy little stuffed moose I bought you eight years ago on a shopping trip in Tahoe City with Uncle Larry, after your first snowboarding broken wrist.

And you were on the cusp of manhood, just opening to maturity. You were making plans for yourself. Your adolescent heart was warming again to your parents. You had only recently experienced the sweetness of romance. You felt you were sexy. How happy we are that you did not leave this earth without tasting the fruit of first love.

You wanted to become a chef, and knew that Tompkins County Community College cooking courses just weren't challenging enough. Three years ago, with your cousins Sarah, Jacob, and Tim, and your sister Rachel as well as many other California relatives, you had dinner at the Culinary Institute of America in Napa—and set your sights on that level of cooking school.

So California was in your dreams for this summer, and you were planning to stay with the Futernicks. Last month I bought a new dresser in anticipation of your visit. Mom told you about this new pine dresser awaiting you, and your face lit up when you heard about it. "Cool," you replied, with Josh-compressed exuberance. Now I will put a framed picture of you atop that chest of drawers.

That will be just one of the seventeen quadrillion ways we will hold your memory. This past Tuesday night, the night you died, a baby lamb was born on Elliot and Rosellen's ranch in Calaveras County. Tim named him Joshua. Your sister Rachel wants to name a son she someday hopes to have...Joshua. Your older sister Leigh will never forget the moment she heard she had a new baby brother.

Darling six-foot, string-beaned, curly-haired, straight-toothed (after four years of orthodontia), husky-voiced, wry-humored, skateboarding, snowboarding, ear-pierced, baggy-pantsed, tee-shirted, SubSpace-gaming, Grass Roots Music Festival–singing, family-adoring, crooked-grinned boy, we will miss you so much.

It is unbearable to think that you're not going to be ambling in the door any moment, surrounded by your usual gaggle of cute, growing-tall, very hungry boys whom you've known and hung out with since fifth grade.

But your spirit truly hovers. There is absolutely no flaw in it, for it is perfected by our eternal love for you and the embrace we still feel of your emerging-to-manhood personality. We send birthday presents of love and peace to you, Joshua George Huffman. Each one of us here had planned to sing Happy Birthday to you.

Instead, we will be reciting Kaddish for you.

This is wrong, so heart-crushingly wrong. But in those words of our ancient tradition, we grace you with the final consoling words of the Kaddish: *May the One who causes peace to reign in the high heavens cause peace to reign down on us*—and, we all add, on you, Joshua—*and on all the world. And let us say, Amen.*

Yes

When Emili asks me mid-day on Thanksgiving if I will officiate
at her wedding in August, my initial impulse is NO. In what feels
like a heartbeat during which so many feelings collide, and before
I answer, I think:

> You are my niece and I love you but I haven't sensed
> you feel close enough to me to bestow this huge honor.
> And because marriage is such an enormous institution
> I have always believed weddings should be performed
> by an official.

I can tell as I look around that your parents are so happy you
have asked me; they are beaming. And suddenly I can't stop
these tears and bury my face in my hands to contain the sobs
and confusion and enormous sense of compliment you have
just paid me, and I think:

> I can shoulder this responsibility but also know
> how much of my life in the coming nine months
> will be taken up wordsmithing marriage—struggling
> to capture the work of a good marriage, diving into the
> layers of the meaning of love. And what you have just
> given me is the gift that you want to get closer to me,
> which is what I have often hoped would happen. And now
> I'm remembering Molly Bloom's gorgeous soliloquy
> ending *Ulysses* and think when I deliver the wedding
> homily I'll end with her yes. And anyway who can say NO
> to such a request and I look at you and yes I happily say
> YES.

Outside

Heavenly Taxonomy

Old-Fashioned Library

A card catalog
with its oak patina,
frayed catalog cards in perfect order.
The metal rod of each drawer soldiering cards in eternal attention.
Creamy stock with decades of ink,
graphite notes conveying a story
about the book it stands in for.

The shelves,
rows of brown or green or red buckram covers.
Decimal-pointed numbers never changing their division.
The heat-impressed foil of 616.86 H98
no matter what library you're in
leads to
The Doors of Perception.

The heavy paper of bound periodicals with their faint smell of clay
a reminder that history can be viewed in rows.

In winter, the toasty odor of radiator heat.

Quiet talk of reader's advisory
co-mingling the desires of librarian and patron,
and the stamp of the date pad
an assurance that those weeks would bring
to a lover of stories
these pages, printed
and bound to touch.

Making

"Life is a process of change and adaptation and making."
            —*Robert Pinsky, at a lecture on poetry and death*

With this enormous brush
art is
making a bed, a coconut cream pie, toast
dinner for two tonight
a fresh pot of coffee
a baby, amends
a mess, the most of a situation
music
a poem
poema—ancient Greek for something made.

Making out: passion with our clothes on,
and making do: the most effortful of all.
Making the bed: straightening sheets and crafting the cradle
Making love in that made or unmade bed.
Making the house spic-and-span.

Making up: a pigmented triumvirate—
pink blush, smoky-lidded eyes, red mouth—
or making up a story for that face
or making up with anyone: herculean with nothing to show, though
making nice requires the hawk's strength as well as the dove's.

Making money, that drumbeat of parents and employers,
can fill the larder or counterfeit economies.
Making a living, infernal voice evolving to
making a life,
moist, propulsive, generative—so familiar we don't notice it.
Every person an artist, every artist a poet
in an ambulatory museum
creating effluvia or masterpieces
lapidary prose or simply a sigh:
making.

Earthquake

OCTOBER 17, 1989, was already feeling like a big day. Not only was it the World Series, the first "Bay Series" between the Oakland A's and the San Francisco Giants, it was Bob's and my twentieth anniversary of meeting each other, which we always celebrate. Typically we'd go out to dinner, but that morning Bob called me at work, suggesting we have a late lunch instead so we could watch the World Series at home that night.

We celebrated at 565 Clay, a beautifully appointed downtown restaurant that no longer exists but was quite popular then. It was owned by a man who also was a Zen priest, so most of the food was exquisite vegetarian. Bob and I each ordered house-made pasta: he had spaghetti with late-harvest tomatoes and I ordered linguine with broccoli, a delicious dish my mother used to make. It seemed a good omen to find it on the menu.

Over lunch Bob and I talked a lot, something we never tired of doing but being parents of young children, rarely got to do over lunch. We reflected on how our love had deepened, how many family and personal storms we had weathered. How lucky we were to have had Jacob, now ten, and Sarah, one week away from turning five, because when we first met and later married, Bob wasn't certain about having children—yet what a loving and engaged father he had become. We each held up our glass of chilled chardonnay and I made a toast: "To my pinch-me good fortune to have met you twenty years ago."

A few hours later, at 4:45, I was in my office at McKinsey & Company.

Bob was on the other end of the phone, calling from the pediatrician's office, saying our daughter Sarah had a clean bill of health. She did not have juvenile diabetes, something we had feared. When Bob's call came from the pediatrician's office, I felt something beyond pinch-me good fortune. I felt pinch-me relief.

I turned to Sarah Maxwell, an Information Specialist with whom I shared an office, and said, "Come on, Sarah. Let's blow this joint. Let's go home and watch the baseball game. After all, you live in Oakland and I live in San Francisco." She thought for a second and said, "Well, OK. I hadn't planned to, but let's go!"

If it was unusual to leave McKinsey at 5:00, it was more unusual for Sarah and me to leave our office together. One of us always worked late, trying to answer some monster reference question from a consultant in San Francisco or Hong Kong or another McKinsey office. (In 1989 there were forty-four McKinsey offices in twenty-two countries.)

The San Francisco Office occupied the forty-seventh and forty-eighth floors of the Bank of America Building at 555 California Street. Even among the gorgeous offices of this pre-eminent management consulting firm, the San Francisco Office was legendary with its panoramic views of the Golden Gate and Bay Bridges, the San Francisco Bay and Pacific Ocean.

Sarah and I cleared our desks, got our purses, and walked out. I closed the sliding glass door behind us. Walking down the hall to the elevator on the forty-seventh floor, I mentioned to Sarah that when Jacob was five, he was already crazy about baseball and loved to watch Giants games on TV with Bob. When he talked about the World Series, he thought it was the World Serious. Sarah laughed.

I pushed the button for the elevator and in a few seconds one stopped. Surprising for that time of day, it was empty. Sarah and I got in, hoping to go straight down to the first floor, not realizing that this elevator was going *up* to the top of the building, the Carnelian Room, an elegant restaurant on the fifty-second floor. Oh well, a few extra seconds wouldn't matter, I thought. At the top floor, the doors opened and a chubby young man and his wife got on the elevator. Given that it was around five o'clock and the guy had a very short haircut and was dressed in shorts, I thought: Must be tourists from the Midwest admiring the view. The doors closed and the elevator descended.

Suddenly the guy seemed to be jumping up and down with such force, such frantic shimmying, I wanted to scream, "What are you *doing*? You're going to break this elevator!" When the elevator started shaking furiously from side to side, I realized something else was going on. "Oh no," I thought. "This elevator really *is* broken."

Before I could say something to Sarah or have another thought, the elevator opened and the four of us were catapulted onto the forty-first floor, the Corporate Office of the Bank of America. The floor and walls shook. Then everything was calm. The walls were intact and the carpet smooth. It was hard to tell if we'd just felt an earthquake but it could have been nothing else.

When the building had opened as the world headquarters of the Bank of America on October 15, 1969—almost exactly twenty years earlier and in fact two days before I met Bob—it was deemed the most seismically sophisticated building in San Francisco. I was told that information on my first day at McKinsey, in the spring of 1981. I was also told that it was (then), at 778 feet high, the tallest building in San Francisco and was used as the site of the movie, "The Towering Inferno."

A bank VP with a transistor radio stashed in his drawer, probably for just such an emergency, turned the radio on. The transistor was placed on his clean desk and about twenty of us huddled around. It seemed like a tiny totem. We were hoping to get news but reporters didn't know much, even though the first effects of the earthquake had been captured on TV during the opening moments of the World Series.

Someone mentioned that in the event of an earthquake certain elevators were programmed to open on the forty-first floor. That explained our sudden, unexpected location, and for twenty-five minutes those of us on the forty-first floor were not allowed to leave. An announcement came over the building loudspeaker saying that *all* emergency doors to the stairs, from all floors, were locked. By now there were about forty people, including those who worked at the Corporate Office, milling around or looking out the windows, trying to get a sense of what had happened in the past ten minutes.

Sarah and I sat on one of the plush corporate couches. We talked a bit but were mainly suspended in our own reveries. I could tell from Sarah's furrowed brow that she was worried. I somehow felt detached from this natural disaster. I was just relieved my daughter didn't have diabetes. When we heard screams coming from a woman trapped in the elevator, our mood turned ominous.

At 5:30 an announcement on the loudspeaker told us the doors were unlocked, stairwell lights were on, and we should proceed down the stairs. Suddenly what seemed like hundreds of people walked down flight after flight. A man wearing a business suit raced ahead of us. He said the Bay Bridge had collapsed, an image too terrible to imagine.

We walked down forty-one flights. Sarah and I and most of the women among us had taken off our shoes, holding them in our hands. Dress-for-work heels weren't meant for such rigor, and I think we just knew they would make an ungodly racket. I felt relieved that my panty-hose were black to match the dark suit I was wearing. They wouldn't show dirt but my feet were getting cold.

When all of us made it to the first floor, Sarah and I saw that we were to exit the Pine Street doors. For a few seconds it felt amazing to be outdoors—to see early evening light and sky, to find the world as we had always known it. Downtown buildings appeared intact. Large shards of window glass, however, were scattered over the sidewalks. I thought: Had I left the building a few minutes earlier I could have been hit by this shower of glass. Later I heard that a woman walking on one of these sidewalks had her arm sliced off by a flying pane of glass.

The air became murky with matter floating down onto the streets. Some buildings had actually bumped into each other, sending poufs of dust into the air, and then returned to their erect standing as though nothing had happened.

Scores of people huddled near street corners, waiting to call home from pay phones. There was something so primal and touching about this need to connect with one's children, parents, spouse. I thought, "E.T., phone home."

After a wait in line, I got a call through to Bob who was at home with Jacob and Sarah. I only had time to hear that he and the kids were OK, and to choke back tears and tell him I was all right, that I would get home somehow even if I had to walk the entire five miles. Sarah tried to call her husband James but he was not at work or at home.

She and I walked the five blocks to BART and Muni, not sure if underground transportation was functioning. By now so many had poured out of downtown buildings that Montgomery Street was overflowing with slightly stunned people. Everyone was quiet and courteous, and you knew a stranger would respond kindly if you asked a question.

As we walked, Sarah and I spoke in hushed tones, echoing the quiet of the streets and people around us. "Did you ever read *The Bridge of San Luis Rey* by Thornton Wilder?" I asked. "I read it in high school. A bridge in Peru collapses and the five people on it fall to their death. It turns out, as you read on, that they all had connections with each other. This feels like that." Sarah answered, "Yes, I read that book in college. I remember being moved by it, too."

It was almost seven o'clock. We reached Montgomery and Market, the location of Sarah's BART station to Oakland and my Muni underground for the N Judah to the Sunset District. I did not ask Sarah to come home with me that night. I knew I should, though I sensed she would say no. My kitchen was filled with dirty dishes from the night before and since Sarah had never been to my home, I felt embarrassed for her to see it in this state. I did, however, think that by now most houses in San Francisco were probably a mess.

On the corner I gave Sarah a hug and said I would call her at home the next day. We knew McKinsey would be closed—and so would every other downtown business, needing time to account for the whereabouts of employees and to determine the extent of structural damage.

A man emerging from the underground told me nothing electrical was running. After taking deep breaths I walked back to California Street to try to catch a bus that ran on fuel. Three packed buses went by without stopping and I was finally able to squeeze onto a lumbering #1 California. No fares were charged, aiding the flow of people onto the bus but the bus itself could barely make it up the steep hill, so filled was it with anxious home-goers who could see, from afar, the Marina up in smoke.

I got off as close to my house as the bus would take me and walked the final mile and a half. I walked first in shoes and then in stocking feet. Streetlights were out, darkening Golden Gate Park, although there was moonlight and an occasional car with headlights passing by. I regretted not having worn brighter colors that day.

Shortly after 9 P.M. I reached my street and put my shoes back on. With my heels clomping on the sidewalk, I ran the final block of Tenth Avenue and bounded up my front stairs. My family was at the open door. For a full minute we cried and I could not stop hugging them, as if we were refugees reunited at some distant border.

Bob had found a few Sabbath candles in the dining room hutch and set them around the living room and kitchen, and on the dining room table. They each became a small circle of light. He also turned on our two flashlights. The rooms looked like a dimly lit campsite, the mess in the kitchen muted by the dark. The effect was almost serene.

Bob and the kids had assessed the damage while it was still light out. There was only one crack in the dining room wall and, upstairs, in Jacob and Sarah's bedroom, a single figurine—Jemima Puddle-Duck—had shattered on the floor.

I heard their stories. Bob and Sarah had been driving home from the pediatrician's office at 5:04. They saw palm and eucalyptus trees in Golden Gate Park bending almost horizontally, with leaves floating everywhere from what seemed like great gusts of wind. Jacob, a fourth grader, had made it home on the school bus and been sitting in the living room by himself, watching cartoons and eating cookies, preparing to switch to the World Series. An entire bookcase near him shook like Jell-O but he thought that was kind of cool.

Bob had already fed the kids and I stood up at the kitchen counter, surveying the dirty dishes, eating Muenster cheese and Stone Wheat crackers and a leg of cold, garlicky chicken. In between bites I could not stop drinking water. After putting Sarah and Jacob to bed, which was not easy because of accumulated fears from the evening, I washed the dishes. Telephones stayed working, but electricity did not return for three days.

The next afternoon I called Sarah Maxwell. She said there had been no BART trains running under the Bay that night and she had spent the night in a downtown hotel with about a hundred other people, all sleeping on the floor of the grand dining room. I felt shame when I heard this. She then said she couldn't talk long because she and James were hoping to get a call from her sister-in-law. Nobody had heard from her.

I called the next day and the next but was unable to reach Sarah. On the third day she answered and told me the news. Her sister-in-law, her favorite among James' siblings, had been entering the freeway on Interstate 880 as the earthquake struck. She was driving onto the Bay Bridge from Oakland at the moment the support columns failed and the upper deck of the freeway crashed onto the lower deck. She was one of the forty-one people crushed to death in their cars.

The Loma Prieta earthquake began at 5:04 P.M. and lasted fifteen seconds, registering 6.9 on the Richter scale. Sixty-three people were killed, nearly four thousand injured, and thousands left homeless. Yet everything is personal, and my experience was detached during that first half hour after the initial shock. Soon, however, the reality of what had occurred overwhelmed me with anxiety and also a sense of awe at experiencing a major earthquake in San Francisco, a city cinematically renowned for earthquakes.

* * *

I have recently re-read *The Bridge of San Luis Rey*. The Foreword to this new edition says that Tony Blair, in the memorial service in New York for British victims of the attack on the World Trade Center, ended his eulogy with the novel's closing sentence: "There is a land of the living and a land of the dead and the bridge is love, the only survival, the only meaning."

Winona Ryder's Shopping Cart

five years before her shoplifting arrest at Bloomingdale's

SHOPPING AT MY neighborhood grocery store, rounding the third aisle, I almost hit her with my cart. Winona Ryder, gazing at dried fruit and grains. She was familiar as daylight despite a camouflage of ordinariness. Her hair hastily tumbled in a ponytail, growing out from highlights. Hi-tops, blue jeans, oversized jacket, no make-up. Still, her wide-set brown eyes were startling.

I was intent on her face but transfixed by her shopping cart. I am a librarian, and cataloging items in her shopping cart was like composing the ultimate catalog card.

The contents of her cart were revealing, as if I'd startled her getting out of the shower. Half and Half, a dozen eggs, butter—hallmarks of a real cook, not an ingenue surviving on celery sticks and Melba toast. She had frozen dinner items, enchiladas, miniature pizzas. I didn't judge.

There may have been a bottle of water, turned so I couldn't read the label, but I imagined the astringent perfume of vodka. Two bananas split like Siamese twins finally separated, three limes, and a baguette wrapped in white paper.

All my life I've looked at grocery carts. Why so a-jitter at this one? Celebrity groceries. Swooning that the star who played Jo in *Little Women*, the book that made me learn to love to read, was two feet away. Someone I'd seen on the huge celluloid screen, pondered in magazine photos, practically sighed for on television, was there. Not only that. She shopped and she cooked.

But like all late-night shoppers trawling under harsh lights, what was most apparent were lines of fatigue. Next to her again, standing in the check-out line, I wanted to tap her shoulder, tell her she is my daughter's favorite actress, that I loved her as Jo. That she should get more sleep, take better care of herself. But of course I didn't.

Heavenly Taxonomy

April on Molokai, walking barefoot under the sky intaglioed with stars,
friends and I pause on the beach after dinner to play a night game.
Star Cards, purchased for this vacation.

I walk next to my friend Penny on an expanse of grass near the ocean.
Normally I resist games but feel open to them under this lavish night sky.

Star Cards: I pull one card from the box Penny is holding,
thin cardboard with random pin holes, but held to the dark light
the holes become a sinewy path. Snake? Dragon?

Yes, *Draco*, Latin for dragon I learn when the name is revealed
on the back of the card. Constellation winding around the Little Dipper.
Draco, one of 48 constellations listed by Ptolemy in the second century,
one of 88 modern constellations like keys on a piano.

The back of the card lists myths attached to Draco: Roman, Babylonian.
Early Christians depicted Draco as the serpent tempting Adam and Eve.

With star card in my hand I should be able to locate the dragon in the sky.
No such luck, the stars themselves resist groupings of anything but
exquisiteness.

Draco was among those star shapes, I know that now
but walking on grass, listening to waves and hearing nothing else,
I escaped all taxonomies and roamed the nameless heavens.

Heart Sandwich

for Sally, my friend of thirty-eight years,
in honor of her marriage to Shelly for forty years

Three plump fabric hearts, one atop another
vertical sachets of East Indian vetiver, fragrant grassy spice
your gift from the Mission District years ago—

our friendship, too, is a heart sandwich tied with a red satin ribbon,
blood coursing through the stout vessel of our friendship
and three-part layering of our own nearly forty years

    when we were each other's succor
    when we lost touch
    when we reconnect now, in an instant.

Those sachets   memory's gift

Vertical pleasures of library shelves
or spicy Tex-Mex meals redolent of your hometown Houston
perhaps the thirty cups of chai we brewed, at least

or the scent of hothouse flowers
your husband brings as offerings
often to soothe a broken heart, his as well as yours

or something for the home, like Herend, Limoges, and Lalique—
all the fragile items we made order of in your house
though that night we talked of the durability of love.

Bring back the baby shower you gave for Jacob
and the one at your home for Nathaniel
adopted, healthy then.

And that day we first met in library school; I thought you knew too much.
Now I know children's literature is the maypole
around which you wrap charm, find humor, place melancholy.
Remember our classroom telling of stories:
me—the exploits of *K'tonton*, Jewish Tom Thumb, his arrival
and riding atop the chopping knife as his mother chopped fish for Sabbath

and you—reciting from memory too
one of Carl Sandburg's *Rootabaga Stories*,
"The Two Skyscrapers Who Decided To Have a Child"

again that verticality
as two buildings lean toward each other
and whisper and decide to have a child, a free child
and it is a train
running free but their child runs into horrible difficulty

still, the skyscrapers stand tall
remain together and, even as they weep
their child completes them, like the three of you
when Nathaniel returns at your door and
hope rises   healing happens   and for a while, health visits.

Lunch Alone on the Deck

Where the bee sucks, there suck I:
In a cowslip's bell I lie.
                    —The Tempest, *V, i*

How eagerly dive the bees in search of pollen
How tempting are the blooms with honeyed promise
The lavender flowers so beckoning and so swollen
The bees suck deep: not just work their work—their bliss.

Outdoors, my bowl offers the same fulfillment
My fork dives in, each tender leaf replete
With soil's gift: the spring's enticing payment
Of sun stored deep, then rain—May's balance sheet.

And as I eat, I listen on the phone
As Lynda K. reads me, "Ourselves or Nothing,"
Her voice so full it's nectared food alone
As Forché's poem yields fruit her reading brings.

How wonderful this noon immersed in threes—
A poem, this late spring lunch, these bees.

Rewriting Hawaii

THERE IS A whispery entrance area in the spa of the Ritz-Carlton Hotel, Kapalua, on the island of Maui, muted tones of slate grey and near-black, lush magenta orchids and slender dracenas. On this day after receiving an exquisite hour-long massage, I request another feedback form from the spa desk clerk. My first version of the feedback, written just this morning but subpar, is full of improving scribbles and overwrites. I don't want to submit this messy card. Yesterday's eighty-minute traditional Lomilomi massage, complete with ancient Hawaiian prayer beforehand, had been so soothing to my sore arms and neck I want to express my gratitude in just the right words.

"I would like another feedback form. I'm a writer," I say to the desk clerk, that declaration slightly augmented from "editor," like lips after a collagen enhancement treatment offered at the spa.

A second draft of a spa feedback form is what a long horizon of Hawaiian relaxation affords me. I had wanted to write on this vacation. Now I want to write a better feedback form. I want to detail my spa experience more carefully, use stronger adverbs, insert tropical imagery. Try to sound poetic and impressive in case somebody cared. I used to be a librarian at a management consulting company and customer satisfaction was a concept taken seriously.

Deborah, a spa employee, larger and taller than I, with bouffant blond hair teased slightly and held in place with a black sparkly headband, looks like Glinda the Good Witch and seems as benevolent in spa-attendee clothes. She has a high, breathy voice and an ever-present smile, nevertheless sincere. She brings me another feedback form and a tall glass of ice water with a floating slice of lemon, asks if she can spray lavender-infused water near my face.

"Yes, of course," I say, thinking this alone is worth the editorial diligence.

"You're a writer," she says in a voice like a confection of spun sugar.

Conspiratorially she adds, "Let me tell you about this contest put on by Celebration of the Arts in Hawaii. It's called, 'Lucky You Live—or Visit—in Hawaii.' You should enter it. I am."

She goes to a cabinet in a corner where files are kept, opens a drawer and brings over a sheet of paper, folded and refolded many times and no longer crisp. She hands it to me and says, "This will be *my* entry. I haven't shown this to anyone." Deborah is standing tall over my shoulder since I am sitting down from trying to create a better feedback card. I read Deborah's five-sentence entry. I know she wants me to say it is wonderful and say, instead, "There are typos and errors I can fix if you'd like." She leaves me alone with her sentences.

A few minutes later she returns and by now I have made corrections and editorial improvements on those eager yet vague sentences, lines with poor syntax and the occasional jolt of incorrect grammar. I first think to myself, "I should be out on the beach, enjoying the cooler morning sun, reading a book or staring into Hawaiian space." But no, not really! I am editing and loving it. I have a new client, pro bono, and am editing a different sort of feedback form—Deborah's entry in a state-run contest saying why she loves Hawaii. Or, rather than a client, I think of Deborah as an English student I might have had but didn't because I never became an English teacher.

"Tell me why you *really* moved to Hawaii," I say looking up, and she now speaks in touching detail. I ask for a clean piece of paper and tell her I will rewrite the entry for her. Sitting in this spa reception area, I who am nearly sixty become Deborah who is twenty-eight. I merge with her dreams and rewrite her version of her life. I did not know her ten minutes ago.

I take her handful of sentences and recraft them into a page-long second draft, including details not anywhere in her original. I write with the same blue pen I brought in for my own feedback-card revision. I add that she is married to her high school sweetheart Jason. They're both from Willamette, Oregon, and have been married seven years. I take details of why I love Hawaii—those gentle trade winds that envelop you the moment you deplane; cloud-filled skies against which palm trees bend in the breeze; those crashing or nearly quiescent waves; whales spouting plume against a fiery sunset; the sweet, non-ironic smile of the Hawaiian people—and blend them with hers.

I include details she just told me of how she loves the fragrance of pikaki and plumeria, how ancient Hawaii welcomes you in, asks your protection and in return grants you the aloha spirit that never leaves. As I am writing she hugs me three times.

This revised entry is what she would have written if she had been me. So, hubris or kindness? Meddling or instruction? I feel elated but should I feel embarrassed? She picks up the page, reads my handwritten blue lines and says, "This is beautiful. I will keep this page forever."

"Type this up and submit this version," I tell her. We hug warmly and say our goodbyes. On my way out I hand the desk clerk my own revised feedback form. I leave thinking that something in what has just happened is a poem. I go and sit at the by-now very warm beach by the Ritz-Carlton and write and rewrite this Hawaiian story.

New Year Poems, Twenty-two Years Apart

New Year—1988 Version

Almost the way
an angler reels in
the catch, we say
"Happy New Year"
as if hope were palpable

At year's end
we tally the grief
the clear relief
eddied around us,
marbling the water
a rotating dun
and deepening

Happy New Year—2010 Version

The way
an angler reels in the day's catch
we say, "Happy New Year"
at Rosh Hashanah
or the very last moment of December.
We usher in the new year
as if happiness
were palpable,
something to long for
and capture,
to view
      net
         deliver.

Toward year's end
we also tally the grieving
the setbacks—some stunning—
as well as the improvements, the risings up,
the breathtaking clarifications.
Every so often
things really do work out.

This quest
for happiness
every day, every new year
tallied against what each in fact brings
is a ledger to be kept only in pencil.
Every year is happy
is unhappy
though a mantra in the brain
tells us happy is what we should be.

It is.
As poet Adrienne Rich insists,
we have to fight
"the temptation to make a career of pain."
Somehow we revive,
sheer survival makes us grasp toward the sun
at times, to feel sun-blessed.

We do this even as difficult truth inserts itself
and love can stall as often as it starts.

We say, "Happy New Year"
and entertain the quest
for ourself and others
tendering a subtle warning
a tender hope
to consider what happiness means
as one year ends and the new one begins,
as time whirlpools around us
marbling the waters,
and we see them muddying
                        clearing
                              deepening.

Work

More Literate Than Numerate

Working Mom

Forty years ago in a music class at college,
taking a midterm, I couldn't unbraid
the three musical lines of the Bach fugue.
They were unruly, so undecodable
I just wanted to lay down my head, forget those lines
and hope I wouldn't get a D.

On a business trip to New York,
in a large hotel bed I dream
of missing the feel of my children's fingers
and speak to no one in particular
of two missed periods,
call them "missed music."

The beat of working days is a troublesome metronome.
Shuffling of words and bodies
taking the N Judah train
walking into commerce,
filling shelves and libraries and ideas
editing books on business
fielding queries from far-flung places
listening to questions
that for all the world sound like a foreign language,
shaking the feeling I had gotten off at the wrong airport.

I want to shout, "You are asking the wrong questions!
You should be wondering about putting food in people's mouths
and how they will face the dark of night."
I never say these words; I try to be dutiful.

At performance reviews I receive praise but my palms sweat.
I know what comes next: *development needs.*

They usually come in threes, like lines of a fugue.
Think and write more like a business person.
Strive for a stronger performance ethic.
Try to get to work on time.

Then the train to rushed shopping, peeling onions, pairing socks,
mopping the floor and sink and faces. Second shift not really
housework, but homework.
And always the need for affection—theirs, mine—
though each clasp (each embrace or kiss) fills
the way caulk repairs a burdened seam.

Children asleep, I sometimes write poetry
try to write this poem.

Mornings after I feel the pull to stay right here
at home in the light,
sipping a cup of tea after my husband and children have left
and I am already late for work.

Analysis

During a break in a course on financial
analysis (which I cannot understand so I write
poems during discussions of issue trees and
return on equity) my friend and I walk around
an imaginary grid, making ever-widening
parabolas as we circle the grounds of the
conference center. We brace our lungs with
bright autumn air, note ochre leaves
shimmering like misplaced fish. I could not
calculate in that classroom but my head clears
with each outdoor breath and I venture
a presentation of my own: *I have watched your*
marriage for years, especially last week-end.
Your husband is desperate I say, wondering
if my voice might observe a trend while
not grasping it (depression eludes paper,
correlates to nothing). *Surely you must see the*
blanket he is under I warn as we complete the
widest band of our track and face each other
squarely. Like all analysis, these words carry
seeds of remorse.

Inventory

MY FIRST JOB was at Midas Muffler Shop in Greensboro, North Carolina. I was fourteen. Before computers, inventory-taking was manual—items were tallied and recorded in pencil, in columns in a ledger. I was hired by my next-door-neighbor, Ken Schneiderman, who owned the shop and needed help counting mufflers at the end of the year. Actually, Ken and his wife Joanie were already my employers since I worked many afternoons and weekend nights babysitting for their two sets of identical twin boys: Steven and Richard, three; and Michael and David, just a few months old.

I wasn't good at the Midas Muffler job, perhaps because it involved the identifying of strange-looking automobile parts and a type of columnar notation that Ken kept trying to teach me and I had a hard time remembering. I would lose my focus and get lost in the counting, or make a notation in the wrong column.

The summer before college I again worked in numbers. I was hired as a temporary bookkeeper at Le Trianon, a French restaurant in San Francisco. Once again I performed poorly because I knew little about bookkeeping. Plus the job was boring. The only good thing was that the restaurant was owned by René Verdon, former chef at the White House during the Kennedy administration. The industrial-sized refrigerators were stocked with leftovers from the night before and our lunches were sensational. Never before had I indulged in vichyssoise, inches-thick rare filet mignon, or tarte tatin.

The following summer I worked as a secretary and bookkeeper at Contour Chair Company in San Francisco. I got that job because Leonard, father of my then-boyfriend Steve, owned the store. Despite wanting to impress my potential future father-in-law, I didn't perform well at this summer job either. My typing skills were poor, I still hadn't learned much about bookkeeping, and it seemed that every week I would forget to call one important supplier or customer.

By now I was beginning to worry about my future employment

prospects. In school I had been a diligent student, adept at grasping ideas and attaching them to facts and figures. Why couldn't I translate this desire to succeed to a *job*? Why was I a work misfit?

During my junior and senior years at U.C. Berkeley, I worked fifteen hours a week at Lucas Books, a well-established bookstore a block from campus. Finally this felt like the right job for me. I adored being surrounded by books, most of them new and used college textbooks. This was bookkeeping I could relate to!

Some afternoons my task would be to shelve textbooks by class, and I'd be transported to a brainy wonderland, imagining what it was like to take that course in twentieth-century European history, invertebrate zoology, or Latin lyric poetry. But most hours I was stationed at the cash register or worked in the map department selling topographic maps. At that time I had never gone on a full-fledged hike, had no idea how hikers used such maps, and would sometimes have to admit to a customer asking a question that I had a learning disability in the reading of maps.

In the summer of 1970, when I left Berkeley twenty-two units short of graduation and went to live with Bob in Grass Valley, I landed a plum job: waitress at The Empress, a Chinese restaurant five miles out of town. This was a sought-after job for people who lived in the boonies, which Bob and I did during the year and a half before we got married.

Late afternoons I would don my maroon polyester shantung uniform, pin up my waist-length hair in a braided bun, be driven by Bob to work because at the time I didn't drive, and then make a sport of counting how many times a night customers would say, "Funny, you don't look Chinese." ("Funny, you're not the first person to say that," I wanted to retort.)

Since feeding people is one of my greatest joys, it was rewarding to serve customers steaming bowls of Won Ton Soup or a house vegetable specialty, Char Su Ding, or other entrees with intricate names cooked by the owner, Joe Leong, who worked solo in the kitchen. I learned that Gewürztraminer was the best wine to accompany Chinese food, and that customers were charmed if I remembered what they ordered the last time they dined or remembered their names. Soon I could tally long checks in seconds, remembering that in the fifth grade I had been good in arithmetic.

But that job had its indignities, too. The other waitress, Kirsten Chow, and I had to arrive at 4:15 to set tables but could not clock in until 5:00. And Joe would not feed us dinner. Kirsten and I had to buy our own food if we wanted to eat, although Joe allowed us to scavenge leftovers on customers' plates brought back to the kitchen. Kirsten and I did this a lot—careful to not eat food that had been clearly forked or chopsticked, or had teeth marks—and felt no shame because we were hungry and wanted to safeguard the little money we'd earn that night.

A few months later I was fired. The reason, Joe told me, was that I was too sassy. When I called Kirsten the next day to tell her the upsetting news, she told me what she'd known for a while. Joe wanted an excuse to hire a new waitress, someone he was having an affair with even though he had a wife and young children. Kirsten's explanation made me feel slightly better (for myself, not for his wife) but getting fired by anyone, especially that sleazebag, carried a sting. I'd wanted to counter that I am *not* sassy but knew *that* would sound sassy, so I spent the next few days crying to Bob and eating almost nothing.

In December 1971, Bob and I married and moved from Grass Valley to San Francisco. Again I was in need of a job and realized, after poring over the Classified Ads in the *San Francisco Chronicle*, that my best bet might be through a job agency. I interviewed at a reputable one, took its screening test and made a perfect score on verbal. Somehow, though, I was placed as a bill collector—a job that sounded awfully downbeat. Nevertheless, I wasn't going to be a bill collector for the phone company or PG&E. Shreve & Company is a fancy jewelry, china, and silver store in downtown San Francisco, similar to Tiffany & Co.

It did not take long before I was unhappy at this job. Using the fake name of Jennifer Adams, I would call customers who were three-months past due on their accounts. People did not have answering machines back then, and I would often have to make five or six calls on my black rotary phone before locating a person at home or at work. I would try to sound friendly, appreciating that this call was embarrassing, and in most cases customers would apologize, explaining that they had forgotten to pay their bill. In a few days their check would appear in the mail and I would take a black pen and ruler and make a line through their name in the monthly book of overdue accounts.

But it was amazing how many sad stories I heard, even in this land of luxury shopping. I would choke up as people told me their tale of woe and have to squelch my urge to say, "Oh, please don't worry. You don't have to pay this bill. I'll put this one in Bad Debt." Occasionally I did that.

I heard stories of spouses who had been killed in catastrophic accidents, customers who'd been diagnosed with stage-four cancer, or people who'd been fired from their jobs and didn't know how they were going to pay their bills, including Shreve's. One distraught woman told me her baby had just been diagnosed with an allergy to food. I knew from her voice she was telling the truth. I still think about that woman and wonder if, and how, her baby survived.

Work. Why had it been so hard for me, especially since I harbored no illusion that someone should be supporting me? Maybe I didn't like leaving my apartment in the morning or didn't like performing tasks I was lousy at. Or didn't like working with numbers, no matter how hard I tried to wrap these jobs in words: trying to speak articulately to customers and peers; writing as well as I could when asked to summarize a sales pitch, capture an account history, or compose a dunning letter, of which I wrote many.

Librarian!

DURING A WEEK'S vacation from Shreve's, I had an epiphany in the middle of a creek.

Bob attended a seminar on book conservation in Sedona, Arizona, given by Colton and Nancy Storm, renowned book conservators. I went along for the trip. Bookbinders, book conservators, and rare book librarians attended the Storms' five-day course. To save money, Bob and I drove to and from Arizona in a yellow Thunderbird we'd borrowed from his dad, camped at a campground in Oak Creek Canyon, and cooked our meals on a Coleman stove. The Sunday before classes began, the Storms had a dinner reception for attendees and I went as Bob's guest. For the first time in my life I met librarians whose specialty was rare books. They spoke with reverence for their work. For the paper and bindings of antiquarian books and for libraries in general.

On Wednesday afternoon, while Bob was at class and I was at our campsite, I took a break from the novel I was reading and decided to crochet a few rows on my half-finished afghan. I never learned to knit but was adept at the simple crochet stitch. For some reason I chose to do my handiwork in the middle of Oak Creek, which was running by our tent. Holding up my afghan so it wouldn't get wet, I waded into the cool shallow water. Sitting on a big rock in the middle of the stream, enjoying the sun and crocheting several rows of the pink and brown afghan I'd brought on this trip for my long hours alone, I looked up from my afghan and said out loud—to the water, really—I'm going to become a librarian!

My mother always said I should be a librarian. Perhaps because I was not career-oriented, never befriended a children's room librarian, and found school librarians to be stern and not very pretty, her suggestion had seemed slightly insulting. That afternoon I knew my mother was right.

Bob and I returned to San Francisco and in a few months I quit my job at Shreve's. March 1972, spring quarter, I returned to Berkeley to graduate, taking all remaining twenty-two units at one time because I could afford only one quarter if I was planning on nearly two years of graduate school. While finishing up at Berkeley I applied to library school, intent on becoming a rare books librarian. This seemed both practical and romantic. After all, Bob's family owned a bookbindery when I met him and he was now studying book and paper conservation. Soon he would become a paper conservator at the Legion of Honor Museum in San Francisco.

I did not get into U.C. Berkeley's School of Library and Information Science, which sent me into my bedroom weeping for hours. Later I took consolation hearing that this program did not usually accept Berkeley undergraduates. And since this school was becoming a frontrunner in digital information technology, I'm sure my wanting to become a rare books librarian puzzled the Admissions Committee. I was accepted at San Jose State's School of Library Science and graduated with an MLS, Masters in Library Science. I never did work with rare books.

Summer 1974. My first job was at Mechanics' Library in San Francisco, a private library founded in 1854 to serve the vocational needs of out-of-work gold miners. This beautiful library with its winding wooden staircases and old glass windows was two blocks from Shreve's. Even though I had an MLS, I was hired for a $6,000-a-year non-professional job. But for that summer I didn't care. After nearly two years of graduate school I was glad to have any job. And there was an unexpected bonus. My father-in-law, Joe Futernick, owned Foster and Futernick Company, which specialized in the rebinding of worn-out books and the binding into volumes of magazines and periodicals. Mechanics' Library was a big customer, so with Futernick as my last name I was a celebrity.

Most hours I worked at the circulation desk, stamping due dates in newly checked-out books, stacking returned books and magazines on a cart, and doing my part to further the incorrect stereotype of what a librarian does. Still, I thrilled to see the books that patrons checked out. A surprising number devoured a weekly diet of seven mysteries, but many members were serious readers of literature.

One patron in particular. I could tell by the books she'd bring to the circulation desk that she was an extraordinary reader. We'd have spontaneous book talks, she on one side and I on the other of the large, semicircular oak desk. She fed me great suggestions: *The Man Who Loved Children*, by Christina Stead; *Miss Leonora When Last Seen*, by Peter Taylor; *The Country Girls*, by Edna O'Brien; and *Père Goriot* because, she said, "Read anything by Balzac."

A few hours a week I'd be released from the circulation desk to shelve books, and these would be my favorite hours. I would go into a literary meditation as I shelved novels in the fiction collection—first by author and then by title—as well as non-fiction volumes with their Dewey Decimal number hand-inked or machine-stamped on the spine. Working at Mechanics' Library was the first job I ever loved.

I knew, however, that I should aspire to a more professional placement and that the paltry salary wasn't sustainable. I applied for, and was hired, at a job that nearly doubled my salary. At $10,000 a year, I worked at Far West Laboratory for Educational Research and Development as a special librarian—a "special library" being a library housed in, and serving, an institution or business.

I missed the old-library beauty of Mechanics', but Far West was a good move because I was finally working as a professional librarian. I oversaw all functions: expanded the book and periodical collection, catalogued, promoted the microfiche on educational research, answered reference questions, improved the look of the library, attended professional conferences, and even supervised two employees. Then, when Ronald Reagan was elected President, funding for educational research evaporated. The internal reference library I managed for six years was shuttered. I was laid off.

More Literate Than Numerate

AFTER BEING LAID OFF at Far West Laboratory, I scrambled again to find a job.

I called the Special Libraries Association Hotline and was intrigued by a posting for a three-month temporary job at McKinsey & Company, a management consulting firm I had heard about from a presentation at SLA. The next morning, a Friday, I called McKinsey and spoke to Linda Kraemer, the Information Specialist (at McKinsey they were not called librarians) managing the interviews. She told me they had pretty much decided on a candidate but I could come in on Monday for an interview. Bring your resume, she told me. I don't have one, I said. I suggest you write one, she answered.

Over the weekend I cobbled together a resume and borrowed a pair of professional-looking shoes from my sister. When I met Linda on Monday we had an unexpected rapport. We were both from New York, Jewish, had the same wedding anniversary, and even had similar last names since my maiden name was Krames.

I had four follow-on interviews, including one with Julien Phillips, a McKinsey partner. He and I conducted this interview at his home in San Mateo with Julien recovering from a herniated disc and flat on his back on his living room couch.

I had a babysitting snafu that afternoon so I took my twenty-two-month-old son Jacob with me. Julien's teenage daughter Lindsey babysat. While her dad and I talked, Lindsey took Jacob for a walk in his stroller, fed him a bottle, and changed his diaper. This was 1981 and I doubt an interview had ever been conducted like this at McKinsey.

There was a five-week lag between my first call to Linda and her calling to offer me the job. And so, on March 18, 1981, I was hired for a three-month job to read, organize, and catalog the massive "dump" of documents from another McKinsey partner, Tom Peters, much of which was backup for a book draft he was struggling to get into shape.

At the beginning of June I gathered my courage and made an appointment to speak to Julien Phillips, whose back was now a lot better. I suggested he hire me for a permanent position. After all, I argued, why would McKinsey want me to walk out the door after reading and synthesizing hundreds of McKinsey and non-McKinsey documents about organizational effectiveness?

He agreed, and I was hired as a full-time librarian (what I called myself) for McKinsey's Organization Practice. On December 31, 2002, I left McKinsey three months short of twenty-two years.

What fell in between was high-octane work. Exhilarating and excruciating, often at the same time. Lots of output and satisfaction coupled with lots of that other part of employment: self-doubt. Yet looking back, I am left with a feeling of gratitude for McKinsey so deep that when I think of the Firm I have to smile. For amazement is what I feel that someone like me—a humanities major in college, former semi-radical at Berkeley in the late '60s and aspiring poet who remembers no algebra—could have lasted at McKinsey. I knew nothing about business.

For example, on my second day my officemate took me to lunch at Le Central. She talked of Siemens, the German company that helped fund the Excellent Company research that was soon to become *In Search of Excellence* (the book draft Tom Peters was working on). When she mentioned Siemens, however, she just mouthed the name. I gave her a blank look and tried to repeat the name. The next second I knew this was a no-no. "You *never* say the names of clients out loud in public!" she practically hissed. My stomach was churning but I couldn't help thinking, Did she just say S-e-m-e-n?

A few months later Bob Waterman, a senior partner and co-author of *In Search of Excellence*, called me into a meeting he was having with his team. He asked for a P&L statement. Once again I gave a blank look. "I don't understand the lingo," I said. If he rolled his eyes I didn't notice. He translated: profit and loss.

Not long afterward Bob Waterman summoned me into his office. "Jennifer, at McKinsey you can only be different on one dimension at a time, and since you'll *always* be different, I suggest you try to dress like everyone else." (I wasn't working directly with clients so I often wore pants to work.) I asked my generous brother Larry to take me shopping at Burberry's. Somehow, though, even on those days when I'd wear the $1,100 navy-blue gabardine suit he bought me, I still felt I was dressing differently.

But in McKinsey parlance, I was adding value. In addition to being a reference librarian, I became the secondary editor of *In Search of Excellence*, the primary editor being John Cox, hired by Harper & Row. Then several months before the book was completed, Tom Peters was fired. His iconoclastic personal style was too rankling to McKinsey and it was a style he had no desire to change.

From May through September 1982, Tom Peters was persona non grata at the San Francisco Office. So he and I would meet like secret agents at the London Wine Bar or the candy shop at the lower level of the Bank of America Building or in my kitchen. We'd go over changes from the editor at Harper & Row, or ones that Bob Waterman or I had made. Other than a few scream-outs larded with the f-word, Tom took these encounters with equanimity and, often, appreciation.

For the year after the book was published (November, 1982), I responded to hundreds of corrections from readers. This level of scrutiny was a surprise since the book was never expected to sell more than its initial 10,000 print run. In fact I won a $100 bet with Tom because he was certain it would never become a bestseller. By May 1983, it had sold a million copies. By 2011, *In Search of Excellence* has sold six million copies and been translated into twenty-seven languages.

Next I helped establish a reference hotline for McKinsey worldwide. I'd listen to a consultant explaining an organizational problem and wonder, "Do you honestly think I, or *anyone*, could answer that?" But by collaborating with colleagues or just thinking for a while, I'd come up with a plan of action for consultants who felt out of their league addressing challenges that were messily human. I'd always been inclined toward helping people and wanted to be a helper at work. Strangely, by becoming a reference librarian in this epicenter of business, I really could be of assistance. Eventually I became an editor for McKinsey, an evolution that was satisfying.

And I traveled, oh Lord, I traveled. Sometimes every week to a meeting in the U. S. or somewhere outside the country. But when I could keep jet lag and missing my family in check, these trips were invigorating. Occasionally, when my attention lapsed during a presentation—or I simply could not parse the language they were speaking—

I would start a poem or dream up a new Op-Ed piece for *The San Francisco Examiner* or go into a reverie about the great novel I'd read the night before in my hotel room.

Not long after my two medical leaves for a repetitive strain injury in my arms—and having many of the partners who respected my work leave McKinsey—my job as editor was eliminated during a series of cutbacks. Each grief waters an old one, and this felt like being fired for being too sassy or not getting the numbers in the right column or being at the whim of a new administration I didn't admire. Or for being, as a McKinsey colleague described me, more literate than numerate.

For months I felt untethered and disheartened, though I spent many days reading and welcomed that pleasure. When the searing pain in my arms and hands began to subside, or at least the pain became more manageable with rest, I decided to start a part-time freelance editing business. With assistance from the California Department of Rehabilitation, I became something I never imagined I'd be, a person with a business. A consultant. Not in business but in writing, though several of my clients write about business. I named my company Third Word Editing. My implicit message to clients: You write two words and I'll write the third.

Value-Added

A DECADE LATER when I decided to complete this manuscript and better understand how I had succeeded and failed in the realm of work, I decided to use McKinsey & Company as my focusing lens. After all, twenty-two years of work life should yield *some* insights and stories. And so I went on a McKinsey quest.

I interviewed ten former bosses and colleagues, expecting to hear the truth, gently stated, about how I did—but mostly did not—fit into the McKinsey culture. I would be speaking to people for whom I maintained fondness and respect, but I had also experienced real strain with several of them during the years we worked together. I therefore entered the walkabout with equal parts anticipation and trepidation.

What came out of those interviews was something so surprising that I'm thankful I took notes. I heard, as we spoke in their office or home, on the phone or in a restaurant (including, with one former director, a restaurant he now owns in St. Helena), how I had influenced their McKinsey experience. How I had helped change the McKinsey culture for the better; how provocative my point of view had been; how "I inhaled" (meaning I, too, came to be imbued with the Firm's performance culture); and how my differentness showed consultants that while facts are very important, I reminded them that organizations are populated with *people*.

Julien Phillips—that dear guy who interviewed me lying flat on his back and later hired me full-time—offered the most touching comment over sushi in my neighborhood. "You were more likely to lead with empathy and intuition, and in doing so, stretched our thinking and strengthened *us* with your respect for this other part of us. In doing that, you helped me and others be presented in the best light."

Words like these have been the greatest gift from the world of work, a world where I have often felt uncomfortable or believed I was not fully welcomed, or in which I have been flummoxed by numbers and those who are good with them. But now that I turn the spotlight on wishing to immerse in words, I see that the world of numbers exists within the world of words that in turn exists within the world of numbers. Each creates an echo essential to the way the human heart and mind work.

I may be more literate than numerate, but the distinction has started to seem less meaningful. After all, good writing has an almost mathematical logic to it and numbers are just another alphabet through which to tell a story.

Immersed in the Printed Word

AFTER MY JOB at McKinsey ended, and while working with doctors and therapists to rehabilitate my arms, I have spent the last decade reading. I have also begun, slowly, to call myself a writer. Many things thrill me, but few thrill me like the printed word.

With two friends I devoted a year apiece to studying Joyce's *Ulysses*, Dante's *Inferno* and *Purgatorio*, and Shakespeare's *Sonnets*. I have taken three one-year Jewish Literature courses and read twenty-four novels by Jewish authors. Every morning I page through *The New York Times* as I eat my toast, buttered and marmaladed if I am feeling indulgent, and drink my tall cup of Murchie's #10 Blend tea.

I take a monthly poetry writing class. As a freelance editor I have worked on five book manuscripts, with clients ranging from a Zen priest–businessman to a public art promoter and peace activist to an electrical engineer and stock market guru.

And because I like to write letters, I write many, on letterhead stationery using my favorite black ink pen, closing the envelope with the feeling I have trafficked in gratitude, consolation, or whenever possible, kindness. I affix a commemorative stamp and run around the corner to the post office, drop the letters in the mail slot. Back home, I await the afternoon mail and hope that someone has sent me a letter, too.

At night I read novels. Or book reviews. I cannot get enough of book reviews in *The New York Times Book Review*, *The New Yorker*, *The New York Review of Books*, even *O Magazine* and *People*. Once again I feel like a librarian, considering all the acquisitions I'll need to round out my collection. Or in the evening's reality I simply contemplate the next book I'd like to read.

I work on improving this manuscript. And now that it will soon go to print, I have to fully take in the notion that I will be a book author. A mother is what I have always wanted to be, but writer is the profession I most admire.

I am swimming in print: others' and my own. I am drowning in *and* breathing in words.

Epilogue

Speak of Love, Reprise

OFTEN, NOW, I play a music box that my son Jacob brought home from Paris as a gift to me when he was in his early twenties. The sentimental melody is "Parlez-Moi d'Amour." I play that music box shamelessly for myself. I listen to it when I still at times feel bewildered or grief-stricken over love—or, even more, when I feel that fabulous, complete sense of loving, and being loved—to remind myself to speak of love. To commit to the primacy of love. To acknowledge that words of love are the words I am most comfortable speaking, and the ones I most long to hear.

Astonishment's Cup

Bring me a perfect pot of tea, thick
    Irish Breakfast my favorite
        though Ceylon promises such travel.

Pour and sweeten the china cup
    with one curve of sugar
        lighten it with an elegant stream of milk.

Stir gently, set the cup down
    watch me as I sip the brew
        a dark ivory I take to my lips.

Though you have never brought me pots of steaming tea
    you serve me astonishment's cup and I
        drink.

I never expected this daughter, this son—these children
    whose hands and hair
        I study as vividly as a master drawing

or this house, whose living room curtains and
    white cotton bedsheets
        feel as familiar as the very skin that enfolds me.

Nor marriage with anyone, certainly not with a man
    able to deflect an argument
        with *sweetheart*.

I never expected this good life,
  you in my bed, handsome, brushing away sadness
    with a fine steady hand.

I never expected this good life,
  you in my bed, and after recurring dreams of loss
    you in the morning, still there.

Acknowledgments

This book would not exist without the loving guidance, deft editorial hand, and generous vision of Lynda Koolish. Lynda took me to my first poetry reading in 1968 and we have been immersed in poetry ever since. Her help and insight are present on every page, and my gratitude is boundless.

As my writing mentor, Michael Lavigne urged me to reveal more of my inner life; I have tried to follow his advice. And then Michael skillfully edited the manuscript, twice.

Annice Jacoby, my fearless partner in words, has also been an ally on this project, pushing me to find broader relevance in my writing.

Two poets offered generous assistance with these poems and stories: Linda Dyer (1960–2006) and Margaret Kaufman.

Jeanne Halpern guided me on many pieces and her final read-through was invaluable, filled with the tough but encouraging feedback an excellent editor delivers.

Kathy Rosenberg-Wohl, Dakin Hart, Terry Horrigan, and Cynthia Scarlett have offered an eye for improvement and their own poetic enthusiasm.

Very special thanks to Hilary Young Brodey who, as birth nurse, helped as I labored with my daughter. As publisher at Capra Press, her faith in my writing helped bring forth this book. Thanks also to Phil Brodey and John and Diana Harrington, also at Capra, for their kind encouragement.

To Julie Heffernan whose beautiful painting graces this book, thank you for letting me use your luminous image and for your inspiration as an artist.

So much of who I am has been formed by the love I received from my parents, Irene and Ben. My heart still brims with gratitude and I honor their memory. From them I also received the priceless gift of my siblings: Larry Krames, Elliot Krames, and Nancy Huffman.

Finally, thank you to the loves of my life: my children Jacob and Sarah—sweeter and dearer than I could ever imagine—and my husband Bob—kindest, wisest, loveliest man I have ever met.

Notes

Four pieces have been adapted or shortened from their original appearance in *The San Francisco Examiner*:

"Carful of Boy, 1994" was published as an Op-Ed, "Happiness for Mom, Former Wallflower, Is a Carful of Boy," on April 2, 1995.

"The Rich Scent of Pine-Sol," a prose poem, was published as an Op-Ed also titled "The Rich Scent of Pine-Sol" on July 6, 1995.

"Winona Ryder's Shopping Cart," a prose poem, was published as an Op-Ed also titled "Winona Ryder's Shopping Cart" on June 23, 1996.

"Harmony Broke Out" has been reworked from an Op-Ed, "After 25 Years, It's Roses," published on February 14, 1997.

"Gone" and "Graveside" were published in a limited edition of *A Small Box of Poets*, Protean Press, 1994.

* * *

On August 22, 2011, as I was putting the final touches on this manuscript, my niece Rachel gave birth to Joshua Natan Moore.